Criminal Law Collection: Condensed Case Files

State v. Edwards
State v. Chapman
State v. Cunningham

Criminal Law Collection: Condensed Case Files

State v. Edwards
State v. Chapman
State v. Cunningham

Hon. Randy Rich

NITA
National Institute for Trial Advocacy

Address inquiries to:
Reprint Permission
National Institute for Trial Advocacy
1685 38th Street, Suite 200
Boulder, CO 80301-2735
Phone: (800) 225-6482
Fax: (720) 890-7069
E-mail: permissions@nita.org

ISBN 978-1-60156-324-8
FBA 1324

14 13 12 11 10 9 8 7 6 5 4 3 2 1

Printed in the United States of America

ASPEN PUBLISHING

Official co-publisher of NITA.
aspenpublishing.com/NITA

Acknowledgements

Dedicated to my mentors, A. Tom Jones and Paul Milich, both of Georgia State University College of Law, who taught me everything I know about jury trials. Also, to my wife Bonnie Rich, a great wife, mom, and cross-examiner.

Note

Electronic exhibits can be found at the following website:

http://bit.ly/1P20Jea
Password: Criminal1

Contents

State v. Edwards

Indictment . . . 3
The Grand Jurors . . . 5
Stipulation of Relevant Dates and Other Issues . . . 7
Supplemental Police Report Prepared By Officer Jack Burquette . . . 9
Supplemental Police Report Statement of Jimmy Peterson . . . 13
Supplemental Police Report Statement of Lanny Cooper . . . 15
First Statement of Michael Edwards . . . 17
Second Statement of Michael Edwards . . . 19
Criminal History of Jimmy Peterson . . . 21
Criminal History of Michael Edwards . . . 23
Criminal History of Lanny Cooper . . . 25
Petition (Delinquent/Unruly) In the Interest of Jimmy Peterson . . . 27
Order of Disposition/Commitment In the Interest of Jimmy Peterson . . . 29
Petition In the Interest of Jimmy Peterson . . . 31
Order of Disposition/Commitment In the Interest of Jimmy Peterson . . . 33
Indictment . . . 35
Sentence . . . 37
Probation Revocation Order . . . 39
Indictment . . . 41
Sentence . . . 43
Indictment . . . 45
Sentence . . . 47
Indictment . . . 49
Petition in the Interest of Michael Edwards . . . 51
Order of Disposition/Commitment In the Interest of Michael Edwards . . . 53
Petition in the Interest of Lanny Cooper . . . 55
Order of Disposition/Commitment In the Interest of Lanny Cooper . . . 57
Petition in the Interest of Michael Edwards . . . 59
Order of Disposition/Commitment In the Interest of Michael Edwards . . . 61
Accusation of Lanny Cooper . . . 63
Sentence of Lanny Cooper . . . 65
Accusation of Michael Edwards and Lanny Cooper . . . 67
Sentence of Michael Edwards and Lanny Cooper . . . 69

Plea of Lanny Cooper 71
Indictment of Michael Edwards and Lanny Cooper 73
U PAWN IT Receipt 75
Crime Lab Report 77
Exhibit 1 – Front of Pawn Shop 79
Exhibit 2 – Front Door 81
Exhibit 3 – Jewelry Case 83
Exhibit 4 – Cash Register 85
Exhibit 5 – Footprints and Victim 87
Exhibit 6 – Victim's Feet 89
Exhibit 7 – Victim's Back 91
Exhibit 8 – Victim's Head 93
Exhibit 9 – Footprints 95
Exhibit 10 – Hat 97
Exhibit 11 – Necklace 99
Jury Charges 101
Indictment Number CR0285 109

State v. Chapman

Indictment 113
The Grand Jurors 115
Stipulations of Relevant Dates and Other Issues 117
Supplemental Police Report Prepared by Officer Jack Burquette 119
Supplemental Police Report Prepared for Internal Affairs by Ben Turner 125
Statement Given to Police Internal Affairs 127
Crime Lab Report 131
Exhibit 12 – Chapman's Car 133
Exhibit 13 – AK-47 Rifle Located in Chapman's Vehicle Trunk 135
Jury Charges 137
Indictment Number CR0286 145

State v. Cunningham

Indictment 149
The Grand Jurors 151
Stipulations of Relevant Dates and Other Issues 153
Supplemental Police Report Prepared for Internal Affairs 155
Supplemental Police Report Prepared for Internal Affairs 159
Statement Given to Police Internal Affairs 161
Statement Given to Police Internal Affairs 165

Exhibit 14 – Cocaine Delivered by Cunningham 167
Exhibit 15 – Exhibit 15 169
Exhibit 16 – Room 103 (On Left), Room 104 (On Right) 171
Exhibit 17 – Hi Restaurant 173
Jury Charges 175
Indictment 181

State v. Edwards

INDICTMENT

Witnesses:

Jimmy Peterson
Darrow County Jail

Detective J.B. Burquette
Darrow County PD

Case No.: CR0285
Superior Court
September Term, YR-0

State of Nita

Versus

Michael Edwards

Offense(s):
1. Malice Murder
2. Felony Murder

True BILL

Carl White

Carl White, Foreperson

Returned in open court by Grand Jury, this 28th day of September, YR-0.

Barbara Underwood

Barbara Underwood, Clerk

The defendant herein waives a copy of indictment, list of witnesses, formal arraignment and pleads

Not guilty.
This 1st day of November, YR-0.

Michael Edwards

Defendant

John Simpson

Attorney for Defendant

Elizabeth Fulton

Prosecutor

IN THE SUPERIOR COURT OF DARROW COUNTY
STATE OF NITA

THE GRAND JURORS selected, chosen and sworn for the County of Darrow, to wit:

1. Carl White, Foreperson
2. Helen Matthews
3. Sally Frank
4. Tim Swenson
5. Mrs. H. T. Turpin
6. Tina Epps
7. Cosmo Kramer
8. Mike Juniper
9. Larry Ferguson
10. Susan Nagel
11. Lora Colander
12. Bruce Harvey
13. Kip Stump
14. Jennifer Wyrick
15. Brad Pitt
16. Mike Mears
17. T. J. Whatley
18. Dabney Pope
19. Dianne Erickson
20. Matt Finklestein
21. Mark Henry
22. Star Shine

Count 1

in the name and on behalf of the citizens of Nita, charge and accuse Michael Edwards with the offense of Murder in violation of Nita Code § 16-5-1(a) in that the said accused, in the County of Darrow and State of Nita, on or about July 15, YR-1, did then and there unlawfully, and with malice aforethought, cause the death of Ray Boyd, a human being, by shooting him in the head, contrary to the laws of said State, the good order, peace, and dignity thereof.

District Attorney
Special Presentment

Count 2

The Grand Jurors aforesaid, in the name and on behalf of the citizens of Nita, further charge and accuse Michael Edwards with the offense of Felony Murder in violation of Nita Code § 16-5-1(c) in that the said accused, in the County of Darrow and State of Nita, on or about July 15, YR-1, did then and there unlawfully cause the death of Ray Boyd, a human being, by shooting him in the head with a handgun, a deadly weapon, during the commission of a felony, to wit: Aggravated Assault; contrary to the laws of said State, the good order, peace, and dignity thereof.

District Attorney
Special Presentment

Stipulations of Relevant Dates and Other Issues

The following facts are stipulated by the parties:

1. The methods and procedures followed by the Nita State Crime Lab are commonly used and relied on by experts in the field. No objections will be made to the procedures used in arriving at the results contained in the crime lab report (contained in statement of witness R. Williams). Crime lab report may be admitted by either party.

2. There is no dispute about the chain of custody of the items tested by the crime lab. No objections will be heard regarding chain of custody.

3. There are no audio recordings or videos of this case.

4. The state must call Detective J. Burquette and Jimmy Peterson and the defendant must call L. Cooper and M. Edwards.

5. The defendant was properly Mirandized by the officers at the time of questioning.

6. All documents included as part of problem materials are certified copies, if applicable, and all signatures reflected therein are authentic.

7. There has been extensive media coverage of this case since the murder of the pawn shop owner and the arrest of the defendant.

8. The time of death is stipulated as 4:00 p.m. EST on July 15, YR-1.

9. The cause of death of Ray Boyd is stipulated as multiple bullet wounds to the head, which were fired from a Smith & Wesson 9-mm handgun. The bullets are stipulated as Remington 9-mm bullets. The bullets were fired from a range of eight inches.

10. The Defendant deposited $100.00 cash into his bank account on July 18, YR-1, through an automatic teller machine (ATM).

11. The included criminal records of all witnesses are accurate and are certified copies.

12. All certified copies of prior convictions are authentic.

13. Michael Edwards's true date of birth is July 15, YR-22.

14. The latent fingerprint recovered from the jewelry case is the fingerprint of Michael Edwards.

15. The pawn ticket is stipulated as a business record.

16. The victim Ray Boyd is in fact Ray Boyd.

17. A preliminary hearing for Michael Edwards was held on July 21, YR-0, in Darrow County Magistrate Court, and Edwards was represented by the Darrow County Public Defender.

18. At the preliminary hearing, Bill Cooper testified to the facts set forth in Officer Jack Burquette's report in case number 03879.

19. The public defender did not cross-examine Bill Cooper.

20. Bill Cooper died August 30, YR-0, of natural causes.

21. Motion to Suppress the search of the defendant's house was heard and denied.

22. No negative inference can be made that the state did not produce the actual handgun in court.

23. GENDER: Burquette is gender neutral; Cooper, Peterson, and Edwards must be played by males.

Supplemental Police Report

THIS REPORT IS PREPARED BY OFFICER JACK BURQUETTE

CASE NUMBER 03879

My name is Jack Burquette. I have been a detective in Darrow County for twenty-six years. Prior to being a detective, I was a uniformed officer for four years. For the last sixteen years I have been the senior investigator in the Crimes Against Persons Division of the police department. I have received training in police work from the Darrow County Police, the Nita Bureau of Investigation, and the Federal Bureau of Investigation.

I first learned of the homicide of Ray Boyd by radio dispatch at approximately 4:05 p.m. on the afternoon of July 15, YR-1. The report was that a body had been found by a customer and a neighboring business owner at the "American U Pawn It" pawn shop located on North Industrial Parkway here in Darrow County. The victim's body was found behind the counter in a puddle of blood. There appeared to be two gunshot wounds to the head. The owner apparently was robbed in connection with the shooting as an entire jewelry case had been emptied. The neighboring business owner witnessed a man entering the store in the minutes before the shooting. The neighboring owner was a white male, age sixty-five, later identified as Bill Cooper. He described the man as wearing an army-style military jacket. The man was a little less than six feet tall, was wearing a baseball hat, and had a long ponytail. Mr. Cooper stated that the hat and hair might have been a Halloween-type costume, which he had seen in stores, that includes a hat attached to long hair. He could not describe why he believed it might have been a costume other than the hair didn't look real. He stated that he was not able to get a good look at the man's face. He later heard two gunshots and heard the back door of the pawn shop slam shut. He never saw the man leave the store. He entered the store, found the body, and called the police. Mr. Cooper was not in good health during the interview. Crime scene photos were taken, and ID was called for possible fingerprints and physical evidence gathering. Several fingerprints were recovered throughout the pawn shop. Subsequent examination revealed that three fingerprints belonged to the victim. One fingerprint that was recovered from the jewelry case was later determined to belong to Michael Edwards.

I was assigned by Chief Harvel to be the lead investigator. The media was notified the following morning, and a request was made for any information. The body was transported for autopsy. The victim was murdered with a 9-mm caliber Smith & Wesson weapon, when two bullets (later identified as Remington projectiles) were fired into the left side of the victim's head at close range. The range was estimated at eight inches by the medical examiner. The time of death was determined to be 4:00 p.m. EST on July 15, YR-1. We had no real leads. There were no other eyewitnesses and very few leads. We began to look through old pawn shop records to see if a particular customer may have been angry and had then come back to take revenge. There was nothing in the records that we believed to be sufficient to warrant further investigation. Other store employees also stated that they did not recall any particular customer who seemed unusually upset in the weeks and months before the shooting.

The only lead we had was that the person who entered the store had left some muddy footprints on the floor after walking through a puddle of water on the floor. Apparently, the air conditioner had been leaking and had caused a puddle in the middle of the floor. A person, possibly the suspect, had walked through the puddle once going to the counter and once leaving the counter area. There were also a series of footprints near the counter and particularly near the jewelry counter, which was empty. The footprints were of no use from a forensic viewpoint because they were muddy and no shoe print pattern could be obtained. We decided to keep this information to ourselves and did not release it to the media. As of August 1, YR-1, no leads were obtained. The case was left open, but inactive due to the lack of leads or suspects.

On July 15, YR-0, one year to the day after the murder, I received a phone call from the Darrow County jail by an inmate named Jimmy Peterson. I had received a number of calls during the last year about the case, but none of the leads had ever checked out. This was the only unsolved murder pending in our county. This call was received at 9:00 a.m. Peterson told me he had information on the pawn shop murder and wanted to meet with me to make a deal. I met with him at the county jail at 10:00 a.m. He refused to tell me the name, but told me that a person in his cell pod had confessed to the murder and had been bragging about it for several weeks. He said that he didn't know which murder it was until he saw it on the television that morning and decided to call police. Before he divulged the name, he wanted a deal on his own criminal charges. Peterson is being held on a sale of crack cocaine charge and has no bond because of his previous criminal record. He is on probation for Possession of Drugs with the Intent to Distribute and is subject to the "two strikes" law on drug dealing. If he is convicted of this charge, he could be sentenced to life in prison. He will be eligible for parole after fourteen years. He was adamant that he wouldn't tell me the name until he was sure he would not get life in prison. I advised him that the district attorney made those decisions, but that I would check on the situation. He stated that he had a lawyer, but preferred not to tell the lawyer what was going on and wanted to make a deal on his own. He later fired his attorney when the attorney advised him not to speak to the police.

What intrigued me about the story was that Peterson knew details about the shooting that only the killer would know. For example, Peterson said he was told that the murderer was afraid he would be caught because of a number of footprints he had left at the scene. He knew about the leaky air conditioner, which jewelry case was empty, how many shots were fired, and the name of the victim. He also stated that the person told him he was wearing a piece of the stolen jewelry when he was booked in at the jail. It was a gold crown necklace. I checked the list of stolen merchandise and found such a necklace was listed with a value of $50.00. Peterson said no one would believe him because of his own criminal record. He told me that he had a drug problem, but that he was not violent and that he was willing to take a polygraph. I don't believe in polygraphs, but when someone will volunteer to take one, that means a lot to me in terms of improving their credibility.

I was very leery of the story because of Peterson's own criminal record. He had a series of drug arrests and served time in jail previously. His last arrest was for drugs and could mean a lot more jail time if he is convicted. He even had a charge for perjury. I talked to the DA's office and spoke to Jerry Moore, ADA. He agreed that the opportunity to solve the murder was probably more important than having a drug dealer go to jail. He agreed to the deal. The deal was for Peterson's drug charges to be held in abeyance in exchange for his cooperation in this case. Peterson will remain on probation from his prior offense, and the deal stipulated that he will be subject to prosecution for the pending drug charge if it is revealed that he was being dishonest with investigators or if he is charged with any other criminal violations while on probation. Furthermore, he is not to be released from prison. He agreed to admit to violating his probation (by using drugs while on probation) and is serving three years in jail.

After going over the deal with Peterson (who had fired his lawyer) and Jerry Moore at the jail, Peterson named Michael Edwards as the cellmate who had confessed to the murder. I went back to the station and ran a computer crime history search. Edwards has a juvenile history of delinquency, shoplifting, and petty theft. He has no history of violence. He was only twenty-one years old at the time of the murder. He has recently been arrested along with his best friend, Lanny Cooper, for stealing Cooper's brother's car. They are both being held and are awaiting trial on the car theft charge. At the time of the murder, Edwards's description was that of a white male, twenty-one years old, and approximately six feet tall.

I decided to interview Cooper first and then Edwards. I had the jail commander separate Peterson, Cooper, and Edwards permanently into different cell pods. Then I spoke to Cooper. He stated that he had heard Edwards talking about the murder of Ray Boyd while in jail, but that Edwards told him that he had made up the story so that no one would hurt him while he was in jail. He stated that he and Edwards had been together on the day of the murder and that he knew Edwards did not do it. He said he clearly remembered the day of the murder, July 15, YR-1, because that was Edwards's birthday. He further stated that Edwards was afraid of Peterson because of his size and criminal record and made up the story about the murder so that Peterson would not bother him. Cooper stated that he had also considered making up a similar story, but decided not to. He said that he would not believe Edwards would murder someone. He stated Edwards and he had used drugs mostly supplied by Edwards, but that he did not know where Edwards got the money for drugs. He stated he knew Edwards had a necklace similar to the one described by Peterson and that he was wearing it the night he was arrested. He said he knew nothing about any footprints or shoeprints and had never heard Edwards say anything about any footprints. I told him he could also be charged as a party to a crime if he was not telling me everything he knew. He said he was through talking and began to cry.

I interviewed Edwards next. He did not have an attorney. I advised him of all his rights, and he stated that he wished to waive his rights and make a statement. I next began to ask him questions about why he was in jail. He told me the story about Cooper's brother, Lanny Cooper, and how he had made out a false report of a stolen car because he and Larry got into an argument. Then I asked him his date of birth; he gave me the date of July 15, YR-22. I asked him what he was doing on his birthday the year before when he turned twenty-one. He stated that he was using drugs at the time and had a big party that night at a local bar with his friends. He stated that he was with Cooper most of the day. I told him that we were tracing some leads in the pawn shop murder and located his name in connection with some property of his that was pawned, but was possibly stolen in the robbery. I told him that we might have recovered some of the property in question. I asked him if he had heard about the pawn shop murder and he stated "only on TV." I asked him if he had ever been to the pawn shop, and he stated, yes, that he had pawned some jewelry there about a week before he turned twenty-one and that he had been "ripped off" by the store manager. He stated he could not remember whether it was Boyd or another employee. He said he pawned some jewelry worth $300.00 for only $50.00 just so he would have some money for drugs. He stated that he had gone to get the jewelry back, but it was stolen in the robbery. I went over the list of stolen items with him, and he mentioned that the "crown" necklace was his and that he would like it returned. He said he had later bought a replacement necklace for $75.00 at another pawn shop. I asked permission to search his home. He gave us permission to search his home.

Before searching his home, I obtained a warrant to inspect the contents of Edwards's belongings at the jail. I located a gold crown necklace that matched the description provided by Peterson and

Cooper. This was the necklace Edwards was wearing on the night of his arrest. I weighed the necklace, and it weighed 2.4 ounces.

ID was called to photograph the home and to look for other possible evidence. We did find a Halloween costume baseball hat with an attached ponytail in his closet. His mother said that he had the costume since he was a boy, but had rarely worn it. We also located two handguns in the home with no serial numbers. He was not charged with these items because we could not determine whether they were in fact stolen. The weapons found in the home matched the description of two of the guns stolen in the pawn shop robbery. They could not be positively matched due to the missing serial numbers. Edwards's mother stated she did not know anything about the guns. The guns were as follows: a .22 caliber Lorcin semi-automatic pistol, and a PPK stainless steel .380 semi-automatic pistol. Neither weapon was loaded. Both were found in a shoebox in Edwards's closet. We also located a small amount of crack cocaine in his bed stand. Edwards was not charged with possession of cocaine since he had been in custody for some time. No further evidence was recovered.

I then went back to the Darrow County jail to question Edwards a second time. I did not tell him what we had found, but only that we had information that linked him to the robbery and murder. He then began to state that he had only made up "that story." I asked him, "What story?" He stated that he had made up the story about him being the murderer because he did not want to appear like a "rookie" in prison. He felt that if people believed that he committed the murder, people would leave him alone. He then stated that he was afraid of one particular inmate named Peterson and had complained of him to the warden. Only after complaining with no response did he make up the story. I asked him what he had heard on "TV" about the footprints at the scene. He stated that he did not know what I was talking about. I asked which jewelry case his necklace was in; he stated he did not know. I then asked him what kind of shoes he had worn on his birthday last year. At that point, he stated he wished to speak to an attorney and the questioning ceased. After discussing the case with Moore, we decided to charge Edwards with murder and armed robbery. Peterson has cooperated fully and will testify at trial. He is still in custody. We have never given a polygraph test to Edwards or Peterson. Edwards was asked if he would take one, but he declined. We would not have given one anyway, but it is important to the investigator if the person is willing to take one. All items were placed into evidence, and the case is now closed. Based on the details relayed by Peterson, Edwards committed the murder. I did not ask Peterson where he was on the day of the murder, but he volunteered that he was out of state in Florida visiting relatives. I have not investigated his alibi because he was not charged. Peterson is a white male, approximately five feet, nine inches tall and has several prominent tattoos on his right arm.

Ann Smith

Sworn and subscribed before me
this 19th day of July, YR-0
Notary Public

Jack B. Burquette

Detective Jack B. Burquette

Supplemental Police Report

STATEMENT OF JIMMY PETERSON

CASE NUMBER 03879

I UNDERSTAND THAT I AM GIVING A STATEMENT TO A LAW ENFORCEMENT OFFICER. I UNDERSTAND THAT ANYTHING I SAY MAY BE USED AGAINST ME IN COURT. I UNDERSTAND THAT I HAVE BEEN ADVISED THAT I MAY HAVE AN ATTORNEY PRESENT AND THAT I HAVE ELECTED TO HAVE MY ATTORNEY PRESENT WITH ME DURING QUESTIONING. I AM SIGNING THIS STATEMENT FREELY AND VOLUNTARILY. I UNDERSTAND AND ACKNOWLEDGE THAT THE CONTENTS OF THIS INVESTIGATION SHALL REMAIN CONFIDENTIAL AND THAT I SHALL MAKE NO MENTION OF ANY PART OF THE INVESTIGATION EXCEPT IN A COURT OF LAW UNDER OATH. I UNDERSTAND THAT I AM NOT ENTITLED TO ANY INFORMATION ABOUT THIS INVESTIGATION FOR ANY PURPOSE.

My name is Jimmy Peterson. I was born in Florida and lived with my aunt because both my parents were killed by police in a shooting at our home. They said my parents were drug dealers and resisted arrest. I was too young to remember. I have been in trouble before. I spent time in juvenile court for raping my neighbor. She was really sixteen, but I guess you're not supposed to do that until you're seventeen. Anyway, I was fourteen. I was put in juvenile hall until I was sixteen. I then left my aunt's house and lived on the street. I was in and out of jail for the next four years. Finally, I moved to Nita. It is cheaper to live here, and the cops are not as smart here. They could never catch me doing anything. I lived off the street when I had money and on the street when I didn't. I would always use drugs and end up back on the street eventually. But I haven't been in trouble for at least ten years. The one thing I didn't know about Nita is this "two strikes" thing for drugs. Drugs have always been my problem, but I shouldn't go to jail for life. I didn't have a choice but to cooperate with police about this investigation. I never wanted to rat on anybody, but you got to look out for number one. My lawyer told me not to say a word because the police would think I did it. I fired him and told him I could cut a deal on my own.

All I know is I heard about the murder after it happened. The murder, the stolen jewelry, all of that was on TV. I was in Florida on the actual day of the murder, but I came back into town the next day. I seen on the papers and all of the television stuff. Back then, I wore my hair in a ponytail, and it was long in the back, so everybody used to say to me "Hey Jimmy, you shouldn't have killed that guy." You know they was just joking. But the police were looking for a guy with a ponytail, so everybody just said that to me a lot. Then a few months later, I got busted again for drugs. I didn't even have that much. I got appointed a lawyer, and he told me that I could get a life sentence with two drug convictions. Man, I was blown away. Anyway, a few weeks later these two young punks came into the jail pod where I'm staying. I always try to scare the new kids because they need to know what it is like before they take a plea. I wish someone had done that to me before I took my plea back then. Anyway, I was roughing both of them up pretty good, really scaring the hell out of them. Nobody ever said anything, so I just kept doing it. The kid then tries to buddy up to me and says he ain't no pansy because he has already "capped" somebody. I didn't believe him. This kid looked like he couldn't hurt a flea. But he said he would tell me about it later. I asked him how he didn't get caught, and he said he was just "lucky" because his footprints and fingerprints were all over the place. At the time, I didn't know he was talking about the pawn shop murder. Over the next few weeks, he told me more and more about the case. Mostly at night when we were alone in the cell together when no one else was around. He said it happened at a pawn shop and that he shot a guy twice. He said he never would have shot him, but he was high and had given the guy some lip about giving him some jewelry back. All he wanted was his necklace, he said. But the store manager said he had to pay $50.00 bucks for it when he only gave him $20.00 a week earlier. He said he was tired of taking crap from this guy. He said he pulled his gun and told the man to bag up the entire jewelry case, which he did. He then said he shot the guy twice and left out the back door. He said he left footprints everywhere because the air conditioner was leaking on the floor. I didn't know it was the pawn shop murder until I saw it on TV on the one-year anniversary. When I heard all of that, I knew this was the kind of information I needed to get out of the slammer. The DA didn't go for it though. I still got stuck with three more years in jail. I will take a polygraph and cooperate fully. If I'm lying or not telling the truth, I could get life for the drugs. If I get in more trouble when I'm out, they turn around and charge me with the drugs. This "deal" ain't that great. I've gotten better deals before. Like when I was in Florida, I got out early after telling the cops about the drugs going on in the jail. They gave me a year off my time and sent me away to the "country club" jail. I guess I should have stayed in Florida.

Ann Smith

Sworn and subscribed before me
this 19th day of July, YR-0
Notary Public

Jimmy Peterson

Jimmy Peterson

- mainly spoke @ night outside the presence of others
- gave more details than he needed to

Supplemental Police Report

STATEMENT OF LANNY COOPER

CASE NUMBER 03879

I UNDERSTAND THAT I AM GIVING A STATEMENT TO A LAW ENFORCEMENT OFFICER. I UNDERSTAND THAT ANYTHING I SAY MAY BE USED AGAINST ME IN COURT. I UNDERSTAND THAT I HAVE BEEN ADVISED THAT I MAY HAVE AN ATTORNEY PRESENT. I AM SIGNING THIS STATEMENT FREELY AND VOLUNTARILY. I UNDERSTAND AND ACKNOWLEDGE THAT THE CONTENTS OF THIS INVESTIGATION SHALL REMAIN CONFIDENTIAL AND THAT I SHALL MAKE NO MENTION OF ANY PART OF THE INVESTIGATION EXCEPT IN A COURT OF LAW UNDER OATH. I UNDERSTAND THAT I AM NOT ENTITLED TO ANY INFORMATION ABOUT THIS INVESTIGATION FOR ANY PURPOSE.

I am Lanny Cooper. My best friend is Mike Edwards, and we were always close. We grew up together in Darrow County. We worked at fast-food restaurants mostly. Our last job was at Pizza Hut on North Industrial Parkway. Not too far from the pawn shop place where that guy was killed. Mike had told me all about it at the time. He had been in a week earlier and had pawned a necklace. He wasn't very happy when he only got $50.00 for it. But he needed the money. Back then we smoked a lot of pot together. No cocaine, only pot. Later, Mike got into cocaine, but he wasn't addicted or anything. Later that week, we went out to celebrate Mike's turning twenty-one. We went to a strip club for lunch and then hung out at O'Malley's from about 2:00 p.m. until late that night. I don't even remember who drove us home. But I was definitely with Mike all day, and we didn't rob nobody. I know I could get in trouble for lying to the police, but I swear to God, we did not do anything other than drink that afternoon. The next day Mike was watching TV and said how that was the same guy who had waited on him at the pawn shop. He got kind of quiet after that. He later told me that he went back to get his necklace, but that it had been stolen in the robbery. I remember a few weeks later he started wearing another gold crown necklace, and I said, "Hey, you found your necklace." He said no, that he had to go out and buy another one. It looked the same to me though. Identical, as far as I could tell. He never even told his mom that he had pawned it, because she had given it to him for his sixteenth birthday.

I remember when we first got to jail, a guy named Peterson kept bothering us. He is mean and kind of weird. He is not from here and would always tell us about all of the crimes he would get into and how he would never get caught. He thinks the police are so stupid because he did a lot worse things, but only got caught for drugs. He thinks the laws are stupid, too, because he could murder somebody and get less time than when he got caught with drugs. He was definitely trying to scare us. We do not belong in jail with convicted felons. We just got in trouble because my brother accused us of stealing his car. It is not true. We had his permission, and my lawyer says we can beat the charge. Neither one of us can make the bond, so we have to wait for court. Peterson kept telling us never to take a plea. One day, Peterson kept asking about the pawn shop murder. It seemed kind of weird at the time, but then the news was saying something about the murder all the time because no one had been caught yet. Then Mike started acting like he did it. Later I asked Mike why he did that, and he said to keep Peterson from bothering him as much. Peterson and Mike are cellmates. Mike has complained about him, but the warden has never done anything. Mike said after he started talking to Peterson about the murder, Peterson left him alone. The only thing was that Peterson would ask him a lot of questions, and Mike would make up stuff. I think he even told him one day that I was involved, too. That is completely false. Neither one of us were involved. That is all I know. I don't know anything about a murder. I don't think Mike would do something like that. I . . . I don't want to say anything else right now.

Ann Smith

Sworn and subscribed before me
this 19th day of July, YR-0
Notary Public

Lanny Cooper

Lanny Cooper

First Statement of Michael Edwards

CASE NUMBER 03879

I UNDERSTAND THAT I AM GIVING A STATEMENT TO A LAW ENFORCEMENT OFFICER. I UNDERSTAND THAT ANYTHING I SAY MAY BE USED AGAINST ME IN COURT. I UNDERSTAND THAT I HAVE BEEN ADVISED THAT I MAY HAVE AN ATTORNEY PRESENT. I AM SIGNING THIS STATEMENT FREELY AND VOLUNTARILY. I UNDERSTAND AND ACKNOWLEDGE THAT THE CONTENTS OF THIS INVESTIGATION SHALL REMAIN CONFIDENTIAL AND THAT I SHALL MAKE NO MENTION OF ANY PART OF THE INVESTIGATION EXCEPT IN A COURT OF LAW UNDER OATH. I UNDERSTAND THAT I AM NOT ENTITLED TO ANY INFORMATION ABOUT THIS INVESTIGATION FOR ANY PURPOSE.

Yeah, I got locked up before. Juvenile court and all that, but this is my first felony. I really should not be here, but Lanny Cooper, my best friend, got charged with stealing his brother's old El Camino. It ain't even worth $100.00, but it is still a felony because it is a car. Anyway, Leonard Cooper made the whole thing up to get even with his brother Lanny for stealing money from him. I got caught in the middle. Lanny's lawyer says the charges will never stick.

My date of birth is July 15, YR-22. When I turned twenty-one, I went pretty wild. I was doing drugs then and had a big party with my friends at a bar that night. I think I spent the whole day with Lanny. If we weren't working, we were usually together at the clubs or watching TV. I remember seeing that pawn shop murder thing on TV. I had just been in there the week before to get some money for some jewelry. When I saw the guy on TV, I knew it was the same guy I had talked to in there a week earlier. It really makes you stop and think. Yeah, I had some jewelry stolen in the pawn shop robbery. I had went in there and sold my gold crown necklace to the guy for $50.00. It was worth a lot more, but I needed the money. I really loved that necklace because it was given to me by my mom when I turned sixteen. I never got it back either. I ended up having to go buy another one because it was stolen in the robbery. I had went up there and checked on it after the shooting, but the store said it was gone. I saw the counter cleared out and everything. There was still blood on the wall when I went in a few days later. It was pretty sick.

Sure, if you can find my necklace that would be great. It is worth probably $300.00. It is solid gold. My new one ain't the same. Yeah, if you want to search my house, it's fine with me, just go ask my mom. I got nothing to hide.

Ann Smith

Sworn and subscribed before me
this 19th day of July, YR-0
Notary Public

Michael Edwards

Michael Edwards

Second Statement of Michael Edwards

CASE NUMBER 03879

I UNDERSTAND THAT I AM GIVING A STATEMENT TO A LAW ENFORCEMENT OFFICER. I UNDERSTAND THAT ANYTHING I SAY MAY BE USED AGAINST ME IN COURT. I UNDERSTAND THAT I HAVE BEEN ADVISED THAT I MAY HAVE AN ATTORNEY PRESENT. I AM SIGNING THIS STATEMENT FREELY AND VOLUNTARILY. I UNDERSTAND AND ACKNOWLEDGE THAT THE CONTENTS OF THIS INVESTIGATION SHALL REMAIN CONFIDENTIAL AND THAT I SHALL MAKE NO MENTION OF ANY PART OF THE INVESTIGATION EXCEPT IN A COURT OF LAW UNDER OATH. I UNDERSTAND THAT I AM NOT ENTITLED TO ANY INFORMATION ABOUT THIS INVESTIGATION FOR ANY PURPOSE.

Yeah, that's my necklace. That's the one that I got to replace the stolen one. The one stolen in the robbery. It was in my stuff when I got locked up. It is smaller than the other one, but they both have a similar crown on them.

I never meant to get involved with this murder thing when I made up that story. I was only trying to fit in with the other guys in here. My cellmate is a guy named Peterson. He would always ask me about the murder at the pawn shop and asked if I had heard anything about it since I am from here. I told him I knew a little and eventually began acting like it was me who did the murder to get some respect out of him. He would constantly intimidate me and act like he was going to hurt me. I told the warden, but got no response. Finally, the story seemed to be the only thing that worked. He kept asking me all of these questions about how I did it. I told him all sorts of stuff. Mostly what I heard on TV. I never said anything about any footprints. I have never heard of that before. I told Lanny Cooper what was going on though. He can tell you that I didn't have anything to do with it. I told him I was making up the story before I even made it up. Plus, Lanny was with me the whole day—July 15—that is the day of my twenty-first birthday for crying out loud. I remember that day like it was yesterday. We all got tanked up at O'Malley's and the strip club. We stayed there from 2:00 p.m. until 12:00 a.m. the next morning. I must have got a cab home because I was really blowing it out. Everybody can tell you that. I was not anywhere near the pawn shop.

Ann Smith

Sworn and subscribed before me
this 19th day of July, YR-0
Notary Public

Michael Edwards

Michael Edwards

Nita Crime Information Center
Criminal History

SUBJECT: JIMMY PETERSON

DATE OF BIRTH: 1/1/YR-35

FOR LAW ENFORCEMENT USE ONLY

Arrest 1:	Rape	7/1/YR-21	
Disposition:	Two Years Custody of Florida DCYS		
Status:	Juvenile Court / Scheck County		
Arrest 2:	Shoplifting	8/29/YR-19	
Disposition:	120 days Juvenile Boot Camp		
Status:	Juvenile Court / Scheck County		
Arrest 3:	Aggravated Battery	5/15/YR-17	Felony
Disposition:	$500.00 Fine / One Year Custody / First Offender Revoked		
Status:	Scheck County / Guilty		
Arrest 4:	Theft by Taking	4/1/YR-16	Felony
Disposition:	Felony Status First Offender Revoked Twelve Months		
Status:	Scheck County Superior Court / Dead Docketed		
Arrest 5:	Armed Robbery	8/15/YR-15	Felony
Disposition:	Dismissed—Cooperation with Federal Authorities		
Status:	Darrow County Superior Court		
Arrest 6:	Burglary / Assault / Possession of Firearm	10/25/YR-15	Felony
Disposition:	Two Years State Penal System / Paroled		
Status:	Darrow County Superior Court / Guilty		
Arrest 7:	Perjury / False Swearing	1/15/YR-12	Felony
Disposition:	Indictment		
Status:	Dead Docketed—Plea in Other Subsequent Case		
Arrest 8:	Sale of Cocaine—Controlled Substances	3/20/YR-10	Felony
Disposition:	Twelve Months Custody—Boot Camp Early Release		
Status:	Darrow Superior Court / Guilty (Possession of Cocaine W/I to Distribute)		
Arrest 9:	Sale of Cocaine—Controlled Substances	5/20/YR-0	Felony
Disposition:	Pending / Sale		
Status:	Darrow Superior Court / No Bond		

NITA CRIME INFORMATION CENTER
CRIMINAL HISTORY

SUBJECT: MICHAEL EDWARDS

DATE OF BIRTH: 7/15/YR-22

FOR LAW ENFORCEMENT USE ONLY

Arrest 1:	Misdemeanor Shoplifting	7/15/YR-6	
Disposition:	Forty Hours Community Service		
Status:	Juvenile Court		
Arrest 2:	Misdemeanor Shoplifting	7/15/YR-5	
Disposition:	Forty Hours Community Service / County Probation / Theft Awareness Program / Two Days Detention RYDC		
Status:	Juvenile Court		
Arrest 3:	Misdemeanor Theft by Taking	3/15/YR-3	
Disposition:	$500.00 Fine / Six Months Probation		
Status:	State Court / Guilty		
Arrest 4:	Theft by Taking / Motor Vehicle	6/1/YR-0	Felony
Disposition:	Pending		
Status:	Nita Superior Court / Bond Set in Amount of $10,000.00		
	Related Defendant: Lanny Cooper		

Nita Crime Information Center
Criminal History

SUBJECT: LANNY COOPER

DATE OF BIRTH: 10/15/YR-23

FOR LAW ENFORCEMENT USE ONLY

Arrest 1:	Misdemeanor Shoplifting	7/15/YR-6	
Disposition:	Forty Hours Community Service		
Status:	Juvenile Court		
Arrest 2:	Misdemeanor Shoplifting	7/15/YR-5	
Disposition:	$500.00 Fine / County Probation		
Status:	State Court / Guilty		
Arrest 3:	Misdemeanor Theft by Taking	3/15/YR-3	
Disposition:	$500.00 Fine / Six Months Probation		
Status:	State Court / Guilty		
Arrest 4:	Theft by Taking / Motor Vehicle	6/1/YR-0	Felony
Disposition:	Pending		
Status:	Superior Court / Bond Set in Amount of $10,000.00		
	Related Defendant: Michael Edwards		

Petition
(Delinquent / Unruly)
In the Juvenile Court of Scheck County, Florida

In the interest of:	Case # 88F-07201
JIMMY PETERSON	Charges: Rape
	Offense Date: July 1, YR-21
	Sex: Male DOB: 1/1/YR-35 Age: 14

TO THE JUVENILE COURT OF SCHECK COUNTY:

1. Your petitioner alleges the child named above to be the sex and age and to have the name there set forth; that the child resides in said county and state with his parent and is in the custody and control of his parents; and that the child is subject to the jurisdiction of this court.
2. That the within petition is filed in the best interest of the public and the within-named child.
3. That said child has violated the section of the code cited below and is a delinquent child by reason of the facts set forth below:

Said child did commit the offense of Rape in violation of §16-6-1 in that said child, in the County of Scheck and State of Florida, on or about July 1, YR-21, did have carnal relations with Rebecca Fitzpatrick, a female, forcibly and against her will.

Petitioner prays that process issue, directed to the parties hereto, requiring them to show cause why said child should not be dealt with according to law.

Wilson Smith, ADA
(Petitioner)

Subscribed and sworn to before me, on information and belief, this 13th day of July, YR-21.

Emma Jones
(Attesting Officer)

The above petition is approved to be filed in the best interest of the public and the named child.

This 13th day of July, YR-21.

Frank Thomas
(Court Designee)

ADMISSION/DENIAL

After having been fully advised of my right to remain silent and my right to have legal counsel, I, Jimmy Peterson, hereby admit / deny the allegations contained in this petition.

This 11th day of October, YR-21.

JJM Foster
(Attorney's Signature)

Jimmy Peterson
(Child's Signature)

Samuel Peterson
(Parent or Guardian's Signature)

Order of Disposition/Commitment
In the Juvenile Court of Scheck County, Florida

In the interest of:

JIMMY PETERSON

Case # 88F-07201

Charges: Rape

Offense Date: July 1, YR-21

Sex: Male DOB: 1/1/YR-35 Age: 14

The above-named child having been adjudicated delinquent of the above-stated offense(s) and in need of treatment, rehabilitation, or supervision, **WHEREUPON**, it is **ORDERED AND ADJUDGED** by the court that said child is hereby:

Committed to the FL DCYS for a period of two (2) years.

So ordered, this 11th day of October, YR-21.

David Green

Judge, Scheck County Juvenile Court

CERTIFICATE

This is to certify that the within and foregoing is a true and correct copy of the original petition, plea, and order of disposition filed of record in the Juvenile Court of Scheck County in Case Number: 88F-07201.

This 21st day of October, YR-0.

Jane Oberton (SEAL)

Jane Oberton, Clerk
Juvenile Court of Scheck County

Petition
(Delinquent / Unruly)
In the Juvenile Court of Sheck County, Florida

In the interest of: Case # 90F-09422

JIMMY PETERSON Charges: Shoplifting

Offense Date: August 29, YR-19

Sex: Male DOB: 1/1/YR-35 Age: 16

TO THE JUVENILE COURT OF SCHECK COUNTY:

1. Your petitioner alleges the child named above to be the sex and age and to have the name there set forth; that the child resides in said county and state with his parents and is in the custody and control of his parents; and that the child is subject to the jurisdiction of this court.
2. That the within petition is filed in the best interest of the public and the within-named child.
3. That said child has violated the section of the code cited below and is a delinquent child by reason of the facts set forth below:

   Said child did commit the offense of Shoplifting in violation of §16-8-14 in that said child, in the County of Scheck and State of Florida, on or about August 29, YR-19, with intent to appropriate merchandise, to wit: Portable Tape Recorder, the property of J.C. Penny Co., a retail establishment, to his own use without paying for said merchandise, did take possession of said merchandise and leave the said retail establishment without paying for same.

Petitioner prays that process issue, directed to the parties hereto, requiring them to show cause why said child should not be dealt with according to law.

Wilson Smith, ADA

(Petitioner)

Subscribed and sworn to before me, on information and belief, this 31st day of August, YR-19.

Emma Jones

(Attesting Officer)

The above petition is approved to be filed in the best interest of the public and the named child.

This 31st day of August, YR-19.

Frank Thomas

(Court Designee)

ADMISSION/DENIAL

After having been fully advised of my right to remain silent and my right to have legal counsel, I, Jimmy Peterson, hereby admit / deny the allegations contained in this petition.

This 23rd day of January, YR-19.

JJM Foster
(Attorney's Signature)

Jimmy Peterson
(Child's Signature)

Samuel Peterson
(Parent or Guardian's Signature)

ORDER OF DISPOSITION/COMMITMENT
IN THE JUVENILE COURT OF SCHECK COUNTY, FLORIDA

In the interest of:	Case # 90F-09422
JIMMY PETERSON	Charges: Shoplifting
	Offense Date: August 29, YR-19
	Sex: Male DOB: 1/1/YR-35 Age: 16

The above-named child having been adjudicated delinquent of the above-stated offense(s) and in need of treatment, rehabilitation or supervision, **WHEREUPON**, it is **ORDERED AND ADJUDGED** by the court that said child is hereby:

Required to complete 120 days of the Juvenile Boot Camp Program

So ordered, this 23rd day of January, YR-19.

David Green

Judge, Scheck County Juvenile Court

CERTIFICATE

This is to certify that the within and foregoing is a true and correct copy of the original petition, plea, and order of disposition filed of record in the Juvenile Court of Scheck County in Case Number: 90F-09422.

This 21st day of October, YR-0.

Jane Oberton (SEAL)
Jane Oberton, Clerk
Juvenile Court of Scheck County

IN THE SUPERIOR COURT OF DARROW COUNTY
STATE OF NITA

STATE OF NITA	)	
	)	
v.	)	Case No. 92CR0937
	)	
JIMMY PETERSON	)	

INDICTMENT

COMES NOW the District Attorney of Darrow County and charges and accuses Jimmy Peterson with the offense of AGGRAVATED BATTERY in violation of § 16-5-24 in that the said accused, in the County of Darrow and State of Nita, on or about May 15, YR-17, did maliciously cause a person, John Fredericks, bodily harm by depriving said John Fredericks of a member of his body, to wit: Right Arm, by breaking it, contrary to the laws of said state, the good order, peace and dignity thereof.

This 14th day of November, YR-17.

John Diaz
DISTRICT ATTORNEY
DARROW COUNTY

The defendant herein waives a copy of indictment, list of witnesses, formal arraignment, and pleads guilty.

This 7th day of December, YR-17.

Jimmy Peterson
Defendant

JJM Foster
Attorney for Defendant

John Diaz
Prosecutor

CERTIFICATE

This is to certify that the within and foregoing is a true and correct copy of the original indictment, guilty plea, original sentence, and revocation order filed of record in the Superior Court of Darrow County in Indictment Number: 92CR0937

This 20th day of October, YR-0.

Rebecca Kline (SEAL)

Rebecca Kline, Clerk
Superior Court of Darrow County

IN THE SUPERIOR COURT OF DARROW COUNTY
STATE OF NITA

STATE OF NITA	)	
	)	
v.	)	Case No. 92CR0937
	)	
JIMMY PETERSON	)	

SENTENCE

The defendant having freely and voluntarily entered a plea of guilty to the charges contained in the within and foregoing indictment, the court hereby sentences the defendant as follows:

The defendant is sentenced to probation for a period of one (1) year and is ordered to pay a fine of $500.00.

This sentence is to be served under the provisions of the First Offender Act.

So ordered, this 7th day of December, YR-17.

Roy Bean

Judge, Superior Court of Darrow County

In the Superior Court of Darrow County
State of Nita

STATE OF NITA	)	
	)	
v.	)	Case No. 92CR0937
	)	
JIMMY PETERSON	)	

PROBATION REVOCATION ORDER

The defendant, having violated his probation in the above-styled case by committing a subsequent offense of Theft by Taking on April 1, YR-16, it is hereby:

Ordered that the defendant's First Offender status is vacated and he is adjudicated guilty of Aggravated Battery and re-sentenced to one (1) year in prison.

So ordered, this 1st day of August, YR-16.

Roy Bean

Judge, Superior Court of Darrow County

IN THE SUPERIOR COURT OF DARROW COUNTY
STATE OF NITA

STATE OF NITA	)	
	)	
v.	)	Case No. 94CR1804
	)	
JIMMY PETERSON	)	

INDICTMENT

Count 1

COMES NOW the District Attorney of Darrow County and charges and accuses Jimmy Peterson with the offense of Burglary in violation of § 16-7-1 in that the said accused, in the County of Darrow and State of Nita, on or about October 25, YR-15, without authority and with the intent to commit a theft, entered the dwelling house of another, to wit: Stephanie Alder, located at 123 Palace Lane, contrary to the laws of said state, the good order, peace, and dignity thereof.

Count 2

COMES NOW the District Attorney of Darrow County and charges and accuses Jimmy Peterson with the offense of Assault in violation of § 16-5-20 in that the said accused, in the County of Darrow and State of Nita, on or about October 25, YR-15, did attempt to commit a violent injury to the person of Stephanie Alder by striking her with his fist, contrary to the laws of said State, the good order, peace, and dignity thereof.

Count 3

COMES NOW the District Attorney of Darrow County and charges and accuses Jimmy Peterson with the offense of Possession of a Firearm in violation of § 16-11-106 in that the said accused, in the County of Darrow and State of Nita, on or about October 25, YR-15, did have on his person a firearm, to wit: a pistol, during the commission of the crime of Burglary, said crime involving the unlawful entry into a building, to wit: 123 Palace Lane, and which crime was a felony, contrary to the laws of said state, the good order, peace, and dignity thereof.

This 21st day of November, YR-15.

Bill Pleasant

District Attorney
Darrow County

The defendant herein waives a copy of indictment, list of witnesses, formal arraignment and pleads Guilty.

This 3rd day of March, YR-14.

Jimmy Peterson

Defendant

JJM Foster

Attorney for Defendant

Bill Pleasant

Prosecutor

CERTIFICATE

This is to certify that the within and foregoing is a true and correct copy of the original indictment, guilty plea, and sentence filed of record in the Superior Court of Darrow County in Indictment Number: 94CR1804.

This 22nd day of October, YR-0.

Cindy Wilson (SEAL)

Cindy Wilson, Clerk
Superior Court of Darrow County

IN THE SUPERIOR COURT OF DARROW COUNTY
STATE OF NITA

STATE OF NITA	)	
	)	
v.	)	Case No. 94CR1804
	)	
JIMMY PETERSON	)	

SENTENCE

The defendant having freely and voluntarily entered a plea of guilty to all counts of the within and foregoing indictment, the court hereby sentences the defendant as follows:

The defendant is sentenced to serve two (2) years on each count in the State of Nita Penal Institution. Each count is to be served concurrently.

So ordered, this 3rd day of March, YR-13.

Jose Fernandez

Judge, Superior Court of Darrow County

IN THE SUPERIOR COURT OF DARROW COUNTY
STATE OF NITA

STATE OF NITA	)	
	)	
v.	)	Case No. 96CR476
	)	
JIMMY PETERSON	)	

INDICTMENT

COMES NOW the District Attorney of Darrow County and charges and accuses Jimmy Peterson with the offense of Violation Nita Controlled Substances Act in violation of § 16-13-30(d) in that the said accused, in the County of Darrow and State of Nita, on or about March 20, YR-10, did unlawfully sell a controlled substance, to wit: cocaine, in violation of the Nita Controlled Substances Act, contrary to the laws of said state, the good order, peace, and dignity thereof.

This 15th day of September, YR-10.

Andy Johnson
District Attorney
Darrow County

The defendant herein waives a copy of indictment, list of witnesses, formal arraignment and pleads guilty.

This 11th day of December, YR-10.

Jimmy Peterson
Defendant

JJM Foster
Attorney for Defendant

Andy Johnson
Prosecutor

CERTIFICATE

This is to certify that the within and foregoing is a true and correct copy of the original indictment, guilty plea, and sentence filed of record in the Superior Court of Darrow County in Indictment Number: 96CR476.

This 21st day of October, YR-0.

Barbara Underwood (SEAL)

Barbara Underwood, Clerk
Superior Court of Darrow County

In the Superior Court of Darrow County
State of Nita

STATE OF NITA	)	
	)	
v.	)	Case No. 96CR476
	)	
JIMMY PETERSON	)	

SENTENCE

The defendant, having freely and voluntarily entered a plea of guilty to the reduced charge of Possession of Cocaine with Intent to Distribute, the court hereby sentences the defendant as follows:

The defendant is sentenced to serve one (1) year, followed by fifteen (15) years probation.

So ordered, this 15th day of December, YR-10.

Patty Clark
Judge, Superior Court of Darrow County

IN THE SUPERIOR COURT OF DARROW COUNTY
STATE OF NITA

STATE OF NITA	)	
	)	
v.	)	Case No. 09CR476
	)	
JIMMY PETERSON	)	

INDICTMENT

COMES NOW the District Attorney of Darrow County and charges and accuses Jimmy Peterson with the offense of Violation Nita Controlled Substances Act in violation of § 16-13-30(d) in that the said accused, in the County of Darrow and State of Nita, on or about May 20, YR-0, did unlawfully sell a controlled substance, to wit: cocaine, in violation of the Nita Controlled Substances Act, contrary to the laws of said state, the good order, peace, and dignity thereof.

This 24th day of June, YR-0.

Andy Johnson
District Attorney
Darrow County

The defendant herein waives a copy of indictment, list of witnesses, formal arraignment, and pleads guilty.

This 24th day of June, YR-0.

Jimmy Peterson
Defendant

JJM Foster
Attorney for Defendant

Andy Johnson
Prosecutor

CERTIFICATE

This is to certify that the within and foregoing is a true and correct copy of the original indictment filed of record in the Superior Court of Darrow County in Indictment Number: 09CR476.

This 21st day of October, YR-0.

Barbara Underwood (SEAL)

Barbara Underwood, Clerk
Superior Court of Darrow County

Petition
(Delinquent / Unruly)
In the Juvenile Court of Darrow County, Nita

In the interest of:	Case # 03J-05200
MICHAEL EDWARDS	Charges: Theft by Shoplifting
	Offense Date: July 15, YR-6
	Sex: Male DOB: 7/15/YR-22 Age: 16

TO THE JUVENILE COURT OF DARROW COUNTY:

1. Your petitioner alleges the child named above to be the sex and age and to have the name there set forth; that the child resides in said county and state with his parent and is in the custody and control of his parents; and that the child is subject to the jurisdiction of this court.

2. That the within petition is filed in the best interest of the public and the within-named child.

3. That said child has violated the section of the code cited below and is a delinquent child by reason of the facts set forth below:

> Said child did commit the offense of Theft by Shoplifting in violation of § 16-8-14 in that the said accused, in the County of Darrow and State of Nita, on or about July 15, YR-6, with intent to appropriate merchandise, to wit: one (1) pair of Nike Tennis Shoes, the property of Sports Authority, Inc., a retail establishment, to his own use without paying for said merchandise, did take possession of said merchandise and leave the said retail establishment without paying for same

Petitioner prays that process issue, directed to the parties hereto, requiring them to show cause why said child should not be dealt with according to law.

Tom Bright, ADA

(Petitioner)

Subscribed and sworn to before me, on information and belief, this 17th day of July, YR-6.

Ohon Jones

(Attesting Officer)

The above petition is approved to be filed in the best interest of the public and the named child.

This 17th day of July, YR-6.

Fran Underwood

(Court Designee)

ADMISSION/DENIAL

After having been fully advised of my right to remain silent and my right to have legal counsel, I, Michael Edwards, hereby admit / deny the allegations contained in this petition.

This 11th day of August, YR-6.

John Simpson
(Attorney's Signature)

Michael Edwards
(Child's Signature)

Phillip Edwards
(Parent or Guardian's Signature)

ORDER OF DISPOSITION/COMMITMENT
IN THE JUVENILE COURT OF DARROW COUNTY, NITA

In the interest of: | Case # 03J-05200

MICHAEL EDWARDS | Charges: Theft by Shoplifting

Offense Date: July 15, YR-6

Sex: Male DOB: 7/15/YR-22 Age: 16

The above-named child, having been adjudicated delinquent of the above stated offense(s) and in need of treatment, rehabilitation or supervision, **WHEREUPON**, it is **ORDERED AND ADJUDGED** by the Court that said child is hereby:

Placed on probation for a period of four (4) months and is required to strictly follow the conditions of probation as set forth below. Failure to strictly follow these conditions could result in revocation of probation and require a hearing before the court, during which the probation could be revoked.

While on probation, the said child shall complete forty (40) hours of community service.

So ordered, this 11th day of August, YR-6.

Augustus Robitus

Judge, Darrow County Juvenile Court

CERTIFICATE

This is to certify that the within and foregoing is a true and correct copy of the original petition, plea, and order of disposition filed of record in the Juvenile Court of Darrow County in Case Number: 97J-05200.

This 21st day of October, YR-0.

Phyllis Thompson (SEAL)

Phyllis Thompson, Clerk
Juvenile Court of Darrow County

PETITION
(DELINQUENT / UNRULY)
IN THE JUVENILE COURT OF DARROW COUNTY, NITA

In the interest of:	Case # 03J-05201
LANNY COOPER	Charges: Theft by Shoplifting
	Offense Date: July 15, YR-6
	Sex: Male DOB: 10/15/YR-23 Age: 16

TO THE JUVENILE COURT OF DARROW COUNTY:

1. Your petitioner alleges the child named above to be the sex and age and to have the name there set forth; that the child resides in said county and state with his parents and is in the custody and control of his parents; and that the child is subject to the jurisdiction of this court.

2. That the within petition is filed in the best interest of the public and the within-named child.

3. That said child has violated the section of the code cited below and is a delinquent child by reason of the facts set forth below:

> Said child did commit the offense of Shoplifting in violation of §16-8-14 in that said child, in the County of Darrow and State of Nita, on or about July 15, YR-6, with intent to appropriate merchandise, to wit: Timex watch, the property of K-Mart, a retail establishment, to his own use without paying for said merchandise, did take possession of said merchandise and leave the said retail establishment without paying for same.

Petitioner prays that process issue, directed to the parties hereto, requiring them to show cause why said child should not be dealt with according to law.

Tom Bright, ADA

(Petitioner)

Subscribed and sworn to before me, on information and belief, this 17th day of July, YR-6.

Ohon Jones

(Attesting Officer)

The above petition is approved to be filed in the best interest of the public and the named child.

This 17th day of July, YR-6.

Fran Underwood

(Court Designee)

ADMISSION/DENIAL

After having been fully advised of my right to remain silent and my right to have legal counsel, I, Lanny Cooper, hereby admit / deny the allegations contained in this petition.

This 11th day of August, YR-6.

Freddie Reynolds
(Attorney's Signature)

Lanny Cooper
(Child's Signature)

William Cooper
(Parent or Guardian's Signature)

Order of Disposition/Commitment
In the Juvenile Court of Darrow County, Nita

In the interest of:

LANNY COOPER

Case # 03J-05201

Charges: Theft by Shoplifting

Offense Date: July 15, YR-6

Sex: Male   DOB: 10/15/YR-23   Age: 16

The above-named child having been adjudicated delinquent of the above stated offense(s) and in need of treatment, rehabilitation, or supervision, **WHEREUPON**, it is **ORDERED AND ADJUDGED** by the court that said child is hereby:

> Placed on probation for a period of four (4) months and is required to strictly follow the conditions of probation as set forth below. Failure to strictly follow these conditions could result in revocation of probation and require a hearing before the court, during which the probation could be revoked.

While on probation, the said child shall complete forty (40) hours of community service.

So ordered, this 11th day of August, YR-6.

Augustus Robitus

Judge, Darrow County Juvenile Court

CERTIFICATE

This is to certify that the within and foregoing is a true and correct copy of the original petition, plea, and order of disposition filed of record in the Juvenile Court of Darrow County in Case Number: 97J-05201.

This 21st day of October, YR-0.

Phyllis Thompson (SEAL)

Phyllis Thompson, Clerk
Juvenile Court of Darrow County

Petition
(Delinquent / Unruly)
In the Juvenile Court of Darrow County, Nita

In the interest of:	Case # 04J-05146
MICHAEL EDWARDS	Charges: Theft by Shoplifting
	Offense Date: July 15, YR-5
	Sex: Male DOB: 7/15/YR-23 Age: 17

TO THE JUVENILE COURT OF DARROW COUNTY:

1. Your petitioner alleges the child named above to be the sex and age and to have the name there set forth; that the child resides in said county and state with his parents and is in the custody and control of his parents; and that the child is subject to the jurisdiction of this court.
2. That the within petition is filed in the best interest of the public and the within named child.
3. That said child has violated the section of the code cited below and is a delinquent child by reason of the facts set forth below:

   Said child did commit the offense of Theft by Shoplifting in violation of § 16-8-14 in that the said accused, in the County of Darrow and State of Nita, on or about July 15, YR-5, with intent to appropriate merchandise, to wit: one (1) pair of Nike Tennis Shoes, the property of Sports Authority, Inc., a retail establishment, to his own use without paying for said merchandise, did take possession of said merchandise and leave the said retail establishment without paying for same.

Petitioner prays that process issue, directed to the parties hereto, requiring them to show cause why said child should not be dealt with according to law.

Tom Bright, ADA

(Petitioner)

Subscribed and sworn to before me, on information and belief, this 16th day of July, YR-5.

Ohon Jones

(Attesting Officer)

The above petition is approved to be filed in the best interest of the public and the named child.

This 16th day of July, YR-5.

Fran Underwood

(Court Designee)

ADMISSION/DENIAL

After having been fully advised of my right to remain silent and my right to have legal counsel, I, Michael Edwards, hereby admit / deny the allegations contained in this petition.

This 15th day of September, YR-5.

John Simpson
(Attorney's Signature)

Michael Edwards
(Child's Signature)

Phillip Edwards
(Parent or Guardian's Signature)

Order Of Disposition/Commitment
In the Juvenile Court of Darrow County, Nita

In the interest of:	Case # 04J-05146
MICHAEL EDWARDS	Charges: Theft by Shoplifting
	Offense Date: July 15, YR-5
	Sex: Male DOB: 7/15/YR-22 Age: 17

The above named child has been adjudicated delinquent of the above stated offense and in need of treatment, rehabilitation, or supervision. **WHEREUPON**, it is **ORDERED AND ADJUDGED** by the court as follows:

It is ordered that said child be and is hereby detained by the Department of Juvenile Justice for care, supervision, and planning as provided by Nita Code § 15-11-35(b) and 49-4A-8, and that the said child be detained for a minimum period of two (2) days in an RYDC.

It is further ordered that said child shall be placed on probation for a period of nine (9) months and is required to strictly follow the conditions of probation as set forth below. Failure to strictly follow these conditions could result in revocation of probation and require a hearing before the court, during which the probation could be revoked.

While on probation, the said child shall complete forty (40) hours of community service, pay a fine of $500.00 and shall complete the Theft Awareness Program.

So ordered, this 15th day of September, YR-5.

Augustus Robitus

Judge, Darrow County Juvenile Court

CERTIFICATE

This is to certify that the within and foregoing is a true and correct copy of the original petition, plea, and order of disposition filed of record in the Juvenile Court of Darrow County in Case Number: 04J-05146.

This 21st day of October, YR-0.

Phyllis Thompson (SEAL)

Phyllis Thompson, Clerk
Juvenile Court of Darrow County

IN THE STATE COURT OF DARROW COUNTY
STATE OF NITA

STATE OF NITA	)	
	)	
v.	)	Case No. 04-C-1332
	)	
LANNY COOPER	)	

ACCUSATION

COMES NOW Elizabeth Fulton, Solicitor-General of Darrow County, and charges and accuses Lanny Cooper with the offense of Theft by Shoplifting in violation of § 16-8-14 in that the said accused, in the County of Darrow and State of Nita, on or about July 15, YR-5, with intent to appropriate merchandise, to wit: one (1) pair of Nike Tennis Shoes, the property of Sports Authority, Inc., a retail establishment, to his own use without paying for said merchandise, did take possession of said merchandise and leave the said retail establishment without paying for same, contrary to the laws of said state, the good order, peace and dignity thereof.

This 25th day of August, YR-5.

Elizabeth Fulton

Solicitor-General
DARROW COUNTY

The defendant Lanny Cooper herein waives a copy of accusation, list of witnesses, formal arraignment and pleads guilty.

This 12th day of November YR-5.

Lanny Cooper

Defendant

Freddie Reynolds

Attorney for Defendant

Elizabeth Fulton

Prosecutor

CERTIFICATE

This is to certify that the within and foregoing is a true and correct copy of the original accusation and guilty plea and sentence filed of record in the state court of Darrow County in Accusation Number: 04-C-1332.

This 21st day of October, YR-0.

Phyllis Thompson (SEAL)

Phyllis Thompson, Clerk
State Court of Darrow County

IN THE STATE COURT OF DARROW COUNTY
STATE OF NITA

STATE OF NITA	)	
	)	
v.	)	Case No. 04-C-1332
	)	
LANNY COOPER	)	

SENTENCE

The defendant Lanny Cooper, having entered a plea of guilty, is hereby sentenced as follows:

The defendant shall be placed on probation for a period of three (3) months and while on probation shall pay a fine of $500.00.

So ordered, this 12th day of November, YR-5.

Fred Adams

Judge, State Court of Darrow County
State of Nita

In the State Court of Darrow County
State of Nita

STATE OF NITA	)	
	)	
v.	)	Case No. YR-6-C-1100
	)	
MICHAEL EDWARDS	)	
LANNY COOPER	)	

ACCUSATION

COMES NOW Elizabeth Fulton, Solicitor-General of Darrow County and charges and accuses Michael Edwards and Lanny Cooper with the offense of Theft by Taking in violation of O.C.G.A. § 16-8-2 in that the said accused, in the County of Darrow and State of Nita, on or about March 15, YR-6, did unlawfully take cash, the property of William Smith, with a value of $250.00, with the intent of depriving said owner of said property, contrary to the laws of said state, the good order, peace and dignity thereof.

This 29th day of April, YR-6.

Elizabeth Fulton
Solicitor-General
Darrow County

The defendant Michael Edwards herein waives a copy of accusation, list of witnesses, formal arraignment and pleads guilty.

This 19th day of June, YR-6.

Michael Edwards
Defendant

John Simpson
Attorney for Defendant

Elizabeth Fulton
Prosecutor

The defendant, Lanny Cooper, herein waives a copy of accusation, list of witnesses, formal arraignment, and pleads guilty.

This 19th day of June, 2006.

Lanny Cooper

Defendant

Freddie Reynolds

Attorney for Defendant

Elizabeth Fulton

Prosecutor

CERTIFICATE

This is to certify that the within and foregoing is a true and correct copy of the original accusation, guilty plea, and sentence filed of record in the State Court of Darrow County in Accusation Number: YR-6-C-1100.

This 21st day of October, YR-0.

Phyllis Thompson (SEAL)

Phyllis Thompson, Clerk
State Court of Darrow County

IN THE STATE COURT OF DARROW COUNTY
STATE OF NITA

STATE OF NITA	)	
	)	
v.	)	Case No. YR-6-C-1100
	)	
MICHAEL EDWARDS	)	
LANNY COOPER	)	

SENTENCE

The defendant Michael Edwards having entered a plea of guilty is hereby sentenced as follows:

The defendant shall be placed on probation for a period of six (6) months, and while on probation shall pay a fine of $500.00.

So ordered, this 19th day of June, YR-6.

Fred Adams

Judge, State Court of Darrow County
State of Nita

IN THE STATE COURT OF DARROW COUNTY
STATE OF NITA

STATE OF NITA	)	
	)	
v.	)	Case No. YR-6-C-1100
	)	
LANNY COOPER	)	

PLEA

The defendant Lanny Cooper having entered a plea of guilty is hereby sentenced as follows:

The defendant shall be placed on probation for a period of six (6) months and while on probation shall pay a fine of $500.00.

So ordered, this 19th day of June, YR-6.

Fred Adams

Judge, State Court of Darrow County
State of Nita

IN THE SUPERIOR COURT OF DARROW COUNTY
STATE OF NITA

STATE OF NITA	)	
	)	
v.	)	Case No. YR-0-CR2406
	)	
MICHAEL EDWARDS	)	
LANNY COOPER	)	

INDICTMENT

COMES NOW the District Attorney of Darrow County and charges and accuses Michael Edwards and Lanny Cooper with the offense of Theft by Taking in violation of O.C.G.A. § 16-8-2 in that the said accused, in the County of Darrow and State of Nita, on or about June 1, YR-0, did unlawfully take a YR-27 El Camino automobile, a motor vehicle, the property of Leonard Cooper, contrary to the laws of said state, the good order, peace, and dignity thereof.

This 15th day of July, YR-0.

Andy Johnson
District Attorney
Darrow County

The defendant herein waives a copy of indictment, list of witnesses, formal arraignment, and pleads guilty.

This 20th day of July, YR-0.

Michael Edwards
Defendant

John Simpson
Attorney for Defendant

Andy Johnson
Prosecutor

CERTIFICATE

This is to certify that the within and foregoing is a true and correct copy of the original indictment filed of record in the Superior Court of Darrow County in Indictment Number: YR-0-CR2406.

This 21st day of October, YR-0.

Barbara Underwood (SEAL)

Barbara Underwood, Clerk
Superior Court of Darrow County

U PAWN IT
781 FULTON INDUSTRIAL PARKWAY
Nita City, Nita 34533
404-555-9087

OPEN 24 HOURS A DAY!

ITEM:	CROWN NECKLACE
	2.4 oz. GOLD
	MISC. GOLD RINGS/JEWELRY (NO VALUE)
VALUE DECLARED BY CUSTOMER:	$300.00
DATE:	6-3-YR-1
CASH AMOUNT:	$20.00
CUSTOMER:	MIKE EDWARDS
	1331 HOPE COURT
	NITA CITY, NITA 34532
CLAIM NUMBER:	33482-009
RECEIVED BY:	R. BOYD
PAWN AMOUNT IF PAID WITHIN 60 DAYS:	$50.00

SIGNED: Michael Edwards

CUSTOMER
BY SIGNING THIS DOCUMENT
CUSTOMER AGREES TO ALL TERMS
AND CONDITIONS STATED HEREIN

CRIME LAB REPORT

CASE NUMBER: YR-1-03879

My name is Paul Garrison. I have been employed with the Nita State Crime Lab for thirteen years. I am a lead technician and laboratory chemist. I have been qualified as an expert in courtrooms across Nita for the last thirteen years. We do all of the forensic work for law enforcement in the State of Nita.

I was asked to examine several pieces of evidence in connection with the above case number. Every piece of evidence is given a unique crime lab identification number when it is received for chain of custody purposes. I received from J. B. Burquette, on July 16, YR-1, the following item:

ITEM NUMBER

Item 39123-08 was a plastic bag containing two bullets labeled "Boyd Autopsy".

TEST RESULTS

Item 39123-08 ballistics analysis shows five grooves to the left, which matches a Smith & Wesson 9-mm caliber semi-automatic pistol. All manufacturers have unique swirl and striation patters on their bullets. Five grooves to the right is Remington. Five grooves to the left is Smith & Wesson. Cannot compare to specific weapon as no gun was recovered.

All of the above tests were completed with approved methods and procedures as provided by the Nita Department of Forensic Sciences, the Nita Bureau of Investigation, and the Nita Crime Lab. All testing was based on scientific procedures that are typically relied on by experts in the scientific community.

Ann Smith

Sworn and subscribed before me,
this 20th day of July, YR-1.
Notary Public

Paul Garrison

Technician Paul Garrison

Exhibit 1

Front of Pawn Shop

Exhibit 2

Front Door

Exhibit 3

Jewelry Case

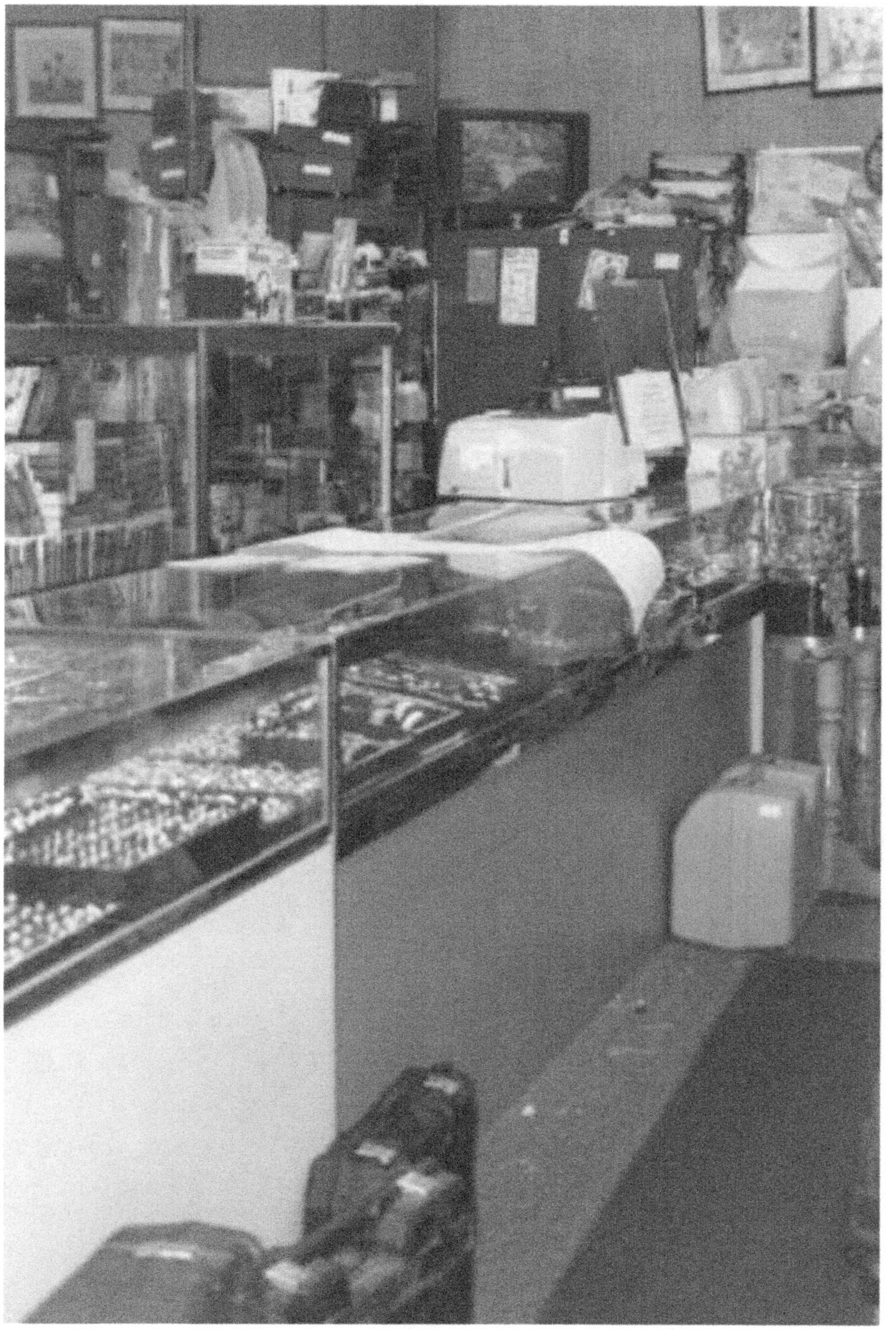

Exhibit 4

Cash Register

Exhibit 5

Footprints and Victim

Exhibit 6

Victim's Feet

Exhibit 7

Victim's Back

Exhibit 8

Victim's Head

Exhibit 9

Footprints

Exhibit 10

Hat

Exhibit 11

Necklace

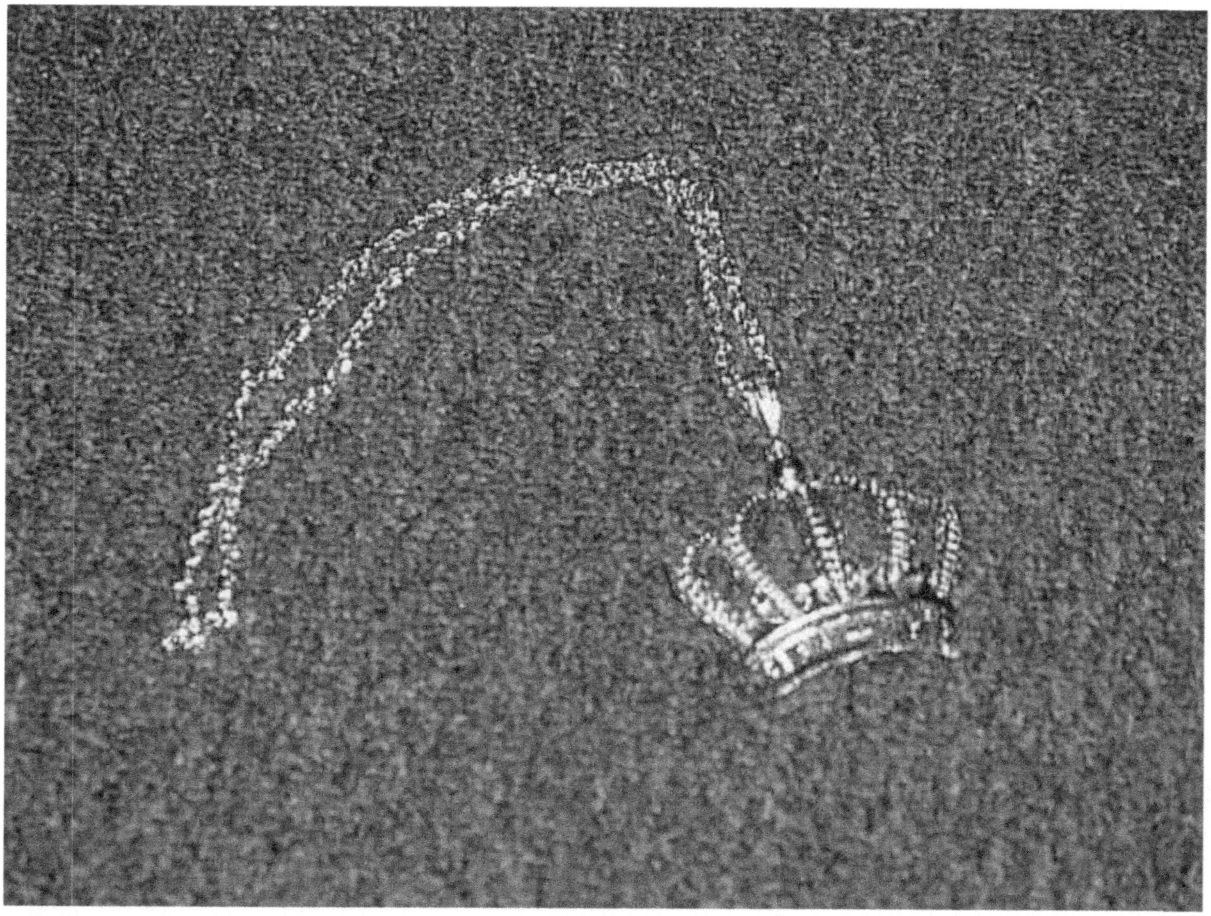

Jury Charges

Indictment and Plea; Not Evidence and Plea; Not Evidence

I caution you that the fact that this accused has been indicted by the grand jury is no evidence of [his] guilt. You should not consider the indictment as evidence or implication of guilt, nor should you consider the plea of not guilty as evidence.

Presumption of Innocence; Burden of Proof; Reasonable Doubt

This defendant is presumed to be innocent until proven guilty. The defendant enters the trial of the case with a presumption of innocence in [his] favor. This presumption remains with the defendant until it is overcome by the state with evidence sufficient to convince you beyond a reasonable doubt that the defendant is guilty of the offense charged.

No person shall be convicted of any crime unless and until each element of the crime is proved beyond a reasonable doubt.

The burden of proof rests on the state to prove every material allegation of the indictment and every essential element of the crime charged beyond a reasonable doubt.

There is no burden of proof on the defendant whatever, and the burden never shifts to the defendant to prove innocence. When a defense (except insanity) is raised by the evidence, the burden is on the state to negate or disprove it beyond a reasonable doubt.

However, the state is not required to prove the guilt of the accused beyond all doubt or to a mathematical certainty. A reasonable doubt means just what it says. It is a doubt of a fair-minded, impartial juror, honestly seeking the truth. It is a doubt based on common sense and reason. It does not mean a vague or arbitrary doubt, but is a doubt for which a reason can be given, arising from a consideration of the evidence, a lack of evidence, a conflict in the evidence, or any combination of these.

If, after giving consideration to all the facts and circumstances of this case, your minds are wavering, unsettled, or unsatisfied, then that is a doubt of the law, and you should acquit the defendant; but, if a doubt does not exist in your minds as to the guilt of the accused, then you would be authorized to convict the defendant.

If the state fails to prove the defendant's guilt beyond a reasonable doubt, it would be your duty to acquit the defendant.

Credibility of Witnesses

You must determine the credibility or believability of the witnesses. It is for you to determine which witness or witnesses you will believe and which witness or witnesses you will not believe, if there are some you do not believe.

In passing on their credibility, you may consider all the facts and circumstances of the case, the witnesses' manner of testifying, their intelligence, their interest or lack of interest, their means and opportunity for knowing the facts about which they testify, the nature of the facts about which they testify, the probability or improbability of their testimony, and of the occurrences about which they testify. You may also consider their personal credibility insofar as it may legitimately appear from the trial of this case.

Conflicts in Testimony

If you find a conflict when you consider the evidence in this case, you should settle this conflict, if you can, without believing that any witness made a false statement. If you cannot do this, then you should believe that witness or those witnesses you think best entitled to belief.

You must determine what testimony you will believe and what testimony you will not believe.

Jury; Judges of Law; Facts

Members of the jury, it is my duty and responsibility to ascertain the law applicable to this case and to instruct you on that law by which you are bound. It is your responsibility to ascertain the facts of the case from all the evidence presented. It then becomes your duty and responsibility to apply the law I give you in the charge to the facts as you find them to be.

Definition of Crime

This defendant is charged with a crime against the laws of this state. A crime is a violation of a statute of this state in which there is a joint operation of an act, or omission to act, and intention (or criminal negligence).

Intent

Intent is an essential element of any crime and must be proved by the state beyond a reasonable doubt.

Intent may be shown in many ways, provided you, the jury, believe that it existed from the proven facts before you. It may be inferred from the proven circumstances or by acts and conduct, or it may be, in your discretion, inferred when it is a natural and necessary consequence of an act. Whether or not you draw such an inference is a matter solely within your discretion.

(Use the following charge with caution in cases involving "specific intent.")

Criminal intent does not mean an intention to violate the law or to violate a penal statute, but means simply to intend to commit an act that is prohibited by a statute.

No Presumption of Criminal Intent

This defendant will not be presumed to have acted with criminal intent, but you may find such intention, or the absence of it, on a consideration of words, conduct, demeanor, motive, and other circumstances connected with the act for which the accused is being prosecuted.

Transferred Intent

If one intentionally commits an unlawful act, yet the act harmed a victim other than the one intended, it is not a defense that the defendant did not intend to harm the actual person injured.

Evidence; Generally

Evidence is the means by which any fact that is put in issue is established or disproved. Evidence includes all the testimony of the witnesses and the exhibits admitted during the trial. (It also includes any facts agreed to by counsel.) It does not include the indictment or the opening statements and closing arguments made by the attorneys.

Direct and Circumstantial Evidence

(Give the following charge in all cases where there is circumstantial evidence.)

(Note: Although there may be exceptions, the Pattern Jury Instructions Committee feels it is a safer practice to give the circumstantial evidence charge in every case.)

Evidence may be either direct or circumstantial or both.

Direct evidence is evidence that points immediately to the question at issue.

Evidence may also be used to prove a fact by inference. This is referred to as circumstantial evidence. Circumstantial evidence is the proof of facts or circumstances, by direct evidence, from which you may infer other related or connected facts that are reasonable and justified in the light of your experience.

To warrant a conviction on circumstantial evidence, the proven facts must not only be consistent with the theory of guilt, but must also exclude every other reasonable theory other than the guilt of the accused.

The comparative weight of circumstantial evidence and direct evidence, on any given issue, is a question of fact for the jury to decide.

(Relative weight of direct and circumstantial evidence is determined by the jury where there are inconsistencies.)

(Where state introduces circumstantial evidence, a charge on the law of circumstantial evidence must be given.)

Bare Suspicion

Facts and circumstances that merely place on the defendant a grave suspicion of the crime charged or that merely raise a speculation or conjecture of the defendant's guilt are not sufficient to authorize a conviction of the defendant.

Alibi

The defendant contends that he was not present at the scene of the alleged offense at the time of its commission. An alibi, as a defense, involves the impossibility of the defendant's presence at the scene of the alleged offense at the time of its commission. Presence of the defendant at the scene of the crime alleged (or defendant's involvement as a co-conspirator or as a party to the crime) is an essential element of the crime set forth in this indictment, and the burden of proof rests on the state to prove such beyond a reasonable doubt.

Any evidence in the nature of an alibi should be considered by you in connection with all the other evidence in the case. If, in doing so, you should entertain a reasonable doubt as to the guilt of the accused, it would be your duty to acquit the defendant.

On the other hand, if you believe from the entire evidence that the defendant is guilty beyond a reasonable doubt, you may convict.

Witness, Impeached by

To impeach a witness is to prove the witness is unworthy of belief. A witness may be impeached by:

a. Disproving the facts about which the witness testified;

b. Proof of general bad character;

c. Proof that the witness has been convicted of a crime involving moral turpitude; or

d. Proof of contradictory statements, previously made by the witness, as to matters relevant to the witness's testimony and to the case.

If it is sought to impeach a witness by "b," "c," or "d," above, proof of the general good character of the witness may be shown. The effect of the evidence is to be determined by the jury.

If any attempt has been made in this case to impeach any witness by proof of contradictory statements previously made, you must determine from the evidence:

a. First, whether any such statements were made;

b. Second, whether they were contradictory to any statements the witness made on the witness stand; and

c. Third, whether it was material to the witness's testimony and to the case.

If you find that a witness has been successfully impeached by proof of previous, contradictory statements, you may disregard that testimony, unless it is corroborated by other creditable testimony, and the credit to be given to the balance of the testimony of the witness would be for you to determine.

Impeachment (Witness)

It is for you to determine whether or not a witness has been impeached and to determine the credibility of such witness and the weight the witness's testimony shall receive in the consideration of the case.

Prior Inconsistent Statement; Substantive Evidence

Should you find that any witness, prior to the witness's testimony in this case from the witness stand, has made any statement inconsistent with that witness's testimony from the stand in this case, and that such prior inconsistent statement is material to the case and the witness's testimony, then you are authorized to consider that prior statement not only for purposes of impeachment, but also as substantive evidence in the case.

Parties to Crime (Defined)

Every party to a crime may be charged with and convicted of commission of the crime.

A person is a party to a crime only if that person:

a. Directly commits the crime; or

b. Intentionally helps in the commission of the crime; or

c. Intentionally advises, encourages, hires, counsels, or procures another to commit the crime; or

d. Intentionally causes some other person to commit the crime under such circumstances that the other person is not guilty of any crime either in fact or because of legal incapacity.

Principal; Failure to Prosecute; Other Involved Persons

Any party to a crime who did not directly commit the crime may be indicted, tried, convicted, and punished for commission of the crime on proof that the crime was committed and that the person was a party to it, even though the person claimed to have directly committed the crime has not been prosecuted or convicted or has been convicted of a different crime or degree of crime or is not amenable to justice or has been acquitted.

Good Character of Defendant

When evidence of the good character of the defendant is offered, the jury has the duty to take that testimony, with all other evidence in the case, in determining the guilt or innocence of the defendant. Good character is a positive, substantive fact and may be sufficient to produce in the minds of a jury a reasonable doubt about the guilt of the defendant. You have the duty to take any evidence of general good character with all the other evidence in the case, and if in doing so you should entertain a reasonable doubt about the guilt of the defendant, it would be your duty to acquit. However, if you should believe the defendant guilty beyond a reasonable doubt, you would be authorized to convict, in spite of the evidence about general good character.

Malice Murder; Defined

A person commits murder when that person unlawfully and with malice aforethought, either express or implied, causes the death of another human being. Express malice is that deliberate intention unlawfully to take away the life of another human being, which is shown by external circumstances capable of proof. Malice may, but need not, be implied where no considerable provocation appears and where all the circumstances of the killing show an abandoned and malignant heart. It is for the jury to decide whether or not the facts and circumstances of this case show malice.

To constitute murder, the homicide must have been committed with malice. Legal malice is not necessarily ill will or hatred, but it is the unlawful intention to kill without justification, excuse, or mitigation.

If a killing is done with malice, no matter how short a time the malicious intent may have existed, such killing constitutes murder.

Nita law does not require premeditation, and no particular length of time is required for malice to be generated in the mind of a person. It may be formed in a moment, and instantly a mortal wound may be inflicted. Yet if malice is in the mind of the accused at the time of the doing of the act or killing and moves the accused to do it, such is sufficient to constitute the homicide as murder.

Premeditation; Defined

(This charge should be given only if a definition of premeditation is requested by the jury.)

Premeditation, as the term is usually used, means a prior determination or plan to commit an act. Premeditation is not an element of the offense of murder and therefore need not be proven by the state to establish malice aforethought. However, any evidence of premeditation, or lack of it, may be considered by you insofar as it relates to the existence, or nonexistence, of malice at the time of the alleged killing.

Felony Murder; Defined

Nita Rev. Stat. §16-5-1(c)

(Note: Felony Murder should not be charged where indictment alleges only Malice Murder, unless indictment also alleges facts showing how murder was committed sufficient to put defendant on Notice of the Underlying Felony.

(Note: If both Malice Murder and Felony Murder are charged, you must instruct the jury to make its verdict clear as to whether they are finding the defendant "guilty of Malice Murder" or "guilty of Felony Murder."

A person (also) commits the crime of murder when, in the commission of a felony, that person causes the death of another human being irrespective of malice. Under our law, (Aggravated Assault) is a felony, and is defined as follows:

(Here give statutory definition of that felony.)

Assault, Aggravated; Statutory Definitions

An assault is:

a. An attempt to commit a violent injury to the person of another; or

b. An act that places another person in reasonable apprehension of immediately receiving a violent injury.

A person commits the offense of aggravated assault when that person assaults another person:

a. With intent to murder, rape, or rob; or

b. With a deadly weapon, or with any object, device, or instrument which, when used offensively against a person, is likely to or actually does result in serious bodily injury.

To constitute an assault, actual injury to the other person need not be shown. It is only necessary that the evidence show, beyond a reasonable doubt, an intention to commit injury on another person, coupled with the apparent ability to commit that injury, or that the other person was intentionally placed in reasonable apprehension of immediately receiving a violent injury from the defendant.

The character of a weapon may be established by direct or circumstantial evidence.

Murder, Felony

If you find and believe beyond a reasonable doubt that the defendant committed the homicide alleged in this bill of indictment at the time the defendant was engaged in the commission of the felony of (Aggravated Assault), then you would be authorized to find the defendant guilty of murder, whether the homicide was intended or not. A person commits (Aggravated Assault) when that person assaults another person with a deadly weapon or with any object, device, or instrument that when used offensively against a person is likely to or actually does result in serious bodily injury. For a homicide to have been done in the commission of this particular felony, there must be some connection between the felony and the homicide. The homicide must have been done in carrying out the unlawful act and not collaterally to it. It is not enough that the homicide occurred soon, or presently, after the felony was attempted or committed. (There must be such a legal relationship between the homicide and the felony so as to cause you to find that the homicide occurred before the felony was at an end or before any attempt to avoid conviction or arrest for the felony.) The felony must have a legal relationship to the homicide, be at least concurrent with it in part, and be a part of it in an actual and material sense. A homicide is committed in the carrying out of a felony when it is committed by the accused while engaged in the performance of any act required for the full execution of the felony.

(The following is a suggested charge to be used after charging both Malice Murder and Felony Murder.)

If you find and believe beyond a reasonable doubt, under all the evidence and the court's instructions, that the defendant is guilty of the offense of murder with malice aforethought, then you must specify such in your verdict, and the form of your verdict in that event would be: "We, the jury, find the defendant guilty of Malice Murder."

If you find and believe beyond a reasonable doubt, under all the evidence and the court's instructions, that the defendant is guilty of the offense of felony murder, then you must specify such in your verdict, and the form of your verdict in that event would be: "We, the jury, find the defendant guilty of Felony Murder."

Motive

Proof of a particular motive is not essential to constitute the crime of murder. Evidence of motive, if any, is admitted for your determination as to whether or not it establishes the state of the defendant's mind at the time of the alleged homicide.

Corpus Delicti

The state is required to prove, beyond a reasonable doubt, that the defendant caused the death of the alleged deceased named in this bill of indictment.

If you believe from the evidence, beyond a reasonable doubt, that the defendant, intentionally, unlawfully, and with malice aforethought, caused the death of the alleged deceased, as and in the manner alleged in this bill of indictment, then you would be authorized to find the defendant guilty.

If you believe that the death of the deceased was caused by some other act or agency with which the defendant had no connection and that the death of the alleged deceased was not caused by the defendant, as and in the manner alleged in this bill of indictment, or if you have any reasonable doubt as to such, then it would be your duty to acquit the defendant.

Verdict (Count 1)

If, after considering the testimony and evidence presented to you, together with the charge of the court, you should find and believe beyond a reasonable doubt that the defendant in Darrow County, Nita, did, on or about (July 15, YR-1) commit the offense of (Malice Murder) as alleged in the indictment/accusation, you would be authorized to find the defendant guilty and, in that event, the form of your verdict would be: "We, the jury, find the defendant guilty of Malice Murder."

Verdict (Count 2)

If, after considering the testimony and evidence presented to you, together with the charge of the court, you should find and believe beyond a reasonable doubt that the defendant in Darrow County, Nita, did, on or about (July 15, YR-1) commit the offense of (Felony Murder) as alleged in the indictment/accusation, you would be authorized to find the defendant guilty and, in that event, the form of your verdict would be: "We, the jury, find the defendant guilty of Felony Murder."

Not Guilty Verdict Form

If you do not believe that the defendant is guilty of either of these offenses, or if you have any reasonable doubt as to the defendant's guilt, then it would be your duty to acquit the defendant, in which event the form of your verdict would be: "We, the jury, find the defendant not guilty."

Unanimous Verdict

Whatever your verdict is, it must be unanimous, that is, agreed by all. The verdict must be signed by one of your members as foreperson, dated, and returned to be published in open court.

Responsibility for Sentencing

(Note: Do not give this charge in death penalty or life without parole cases.)

You are only concerned with the guilt or innocence of the defendant. You are not to concern yourselves with punishment.

Deliberations

One of your first duties in the jury room will be to select one of your number to act as foreperson, who will preside over your deliberations and who will sign the verdict to which all twelve of you freely and voluntarily agree.

You should start your deliberations with an open mind. Consult with one another and consider each other's views. Each of you must decide this case for yourself, but you should do so only after a discussion and consideration of the case with your fellow jurors. Do not hesitate to change an opinion if convinced that it is wrong. However, you should never surrender an honest opinion to be congenial or to reach a verdict solely because of the opinions of the other jurors.

Court Has No Interest in Case

By no ruling or comment the court has made during the progress of the trial has the court intended to express any opinion on the facts of this case, the credibility of the witnesses, the evidence, or the guilt or innocence of the defendant.

IN THE SUPERIOR COURT OF DARROW COUNTY
STATE OF NITA

STATE OF NITA	)	
	)	
	)	
	)	INDICTMENT NUMBER: CR0285
v.	)	
	)	
	)	YR-0-CR0285
	)	
MICHAEL EDWARDS	)	
DEFENDANT	)	

VERDICT

COUNT 1

AS TO COUNT 1, WE THE JURY FIND THE DEFENDANT: ______________________________

COUNT 2

AS TO COUNT 2, WE THE JURY FIND THE DEFENDANT: ______________________________

THIS _____ DAY OF _____, YR-_____.

____

FOREPERSON

State v. Chapman

INDICTMENT

Witnesses:

Detective Ben Turner
Darrow County PD

Detective J.B. Burquette
Darrow County PD

Case No.: CR0286
Superior Court
August Term, YR-0

State of Nita

Versus

Alex Chapman

Offense(s):
1. Malice Murder
2. Felony Murder

True BILL

Carl White

Carl White, Foreperson

Returned in open court by Grand Jury,
This 28th day of August, YR-0.

Barbara Underwood

Barbara Underwood, Clerk

The defendant herein waives a copy of indictment, list of witnesses, formal arraignment and pleads _Not_ guilty.

This 1st day of November, YR-0.

Alex Chapman

Defendant

Lisa Watkins

Attorney for Defendant

Elizabeth Fulton

Prosecutor

IN THE SUPERIOR COURT OF DARROW COUNTY
STATE OF NITA

THE GRAND JURORS selected, chosen, and sworn for the County of Darrow, to wit:

1. Carl White, Foreperson
2. Helen Matthews
3. Sally Frank
4. Tim Swenson
5. Mrs. H. T. Turpin
6. Tina Epps
7. Cosmo Kramer
8. Mike Juniper
9. Larry Ferguson
10. Susan Nagel
11. Lora Colander
12. Bruce Harvey
13. Kip Stump
14. Jennifer Wyrick
15. Brad Pitt
16. Mike Mears
17. T. J. Whatley
18. Dabney Pope
19. Dianne Erickson
20. Matt Finklestein
21. Mark Henry
22. Star Shine

Count 1

in the name and behalf of the citizens of Nita, charge and accuse Alex Chapman with the offense of Murder in violation of Nita Code § 16-5-1(a) in that the said accused, in the County of Darrow and State of Nita, on or about July 15, YR-1, did then and there unlawfully, and with malice aforethought, cause the death of Emma Jeans, a human being, by shooting her in the head, contrary to the laws of said state, the good order, peace, and dignity thereof.

District Attorney
Special Presentment

Count 2

The Grand Jurors aforesaid, in the name and behalf of the citizens of Nita, further charge and accuse Alex Chapman with the offense of Felony Murder in violation of Nita Code § 16-5-1(c) in that the said accused, in the County of Darrow and State of Nita, on or about July 15, YR-1, did then and there unlawfully cause the death of Emma Jeans, a human being, by shooting her in the head with a handgun, a deadly weapon, during the commission of a felony, to wit: Aggravated Assault; contrary to the laws of said state, the good order, peace, and dignity thereof.

District Attorney
Special Presentment

STIPULATIONS OF RELEVANT DATES AND OTHER ISSUES

The following events occurred on the following dates:

1. July 15, YR-1 The victim murdered in Darrow County.
2. July 17, YR-1 The defendant arrested.
3. August 28, YR-1 The defendant indicted.
4. August 30, YR-1 Internal Affairs investigation issues sealed report to District Attorney
5. May 20, YR-0 Order issued by Superior Court of Darrow County regarding Motion to Reveal Contents of Internal Affairs investigation. Court finds that some witness statements are relevant and orders portions of the record released to the defendant (all released documents are included in problem materials). Due to pending indictment in this case, remainder of materials remains sealed by Superior Court order.
6. November 16, YR-0 Trial of the defendant.

The following facts are stipulated by the parties:

1. The methods and procedures followed by the state crime lab are commonly used and relied on by experts in the field. No objections will be made to the procedures used in arriving at the results contained in the crime lab report (contained in statement of witness, Paul Garrison).
2. There is no dispute as to the chain of custody of the items tested by the crime lab. No objections will be heard regarding chain of custody.
3. There are no audio or video recordings of this case.
4. The defendant must be male. The state must call Detective J. B. Burquette and Paul Garrison.
5. The defense must call Alex Chapman and Ben Turner.
6. The muffler shop in question is located in Darrow County.
7. The defendant was properly Mirandized by the officers at the time of questioning.
8. All documents included as part of problem materials are certified copies, if applicable.
9. There has been extensive media coverage of this case since the arrest of the defendant.

10. The muffler shop is located nine miles from the precinct. The defendant lives eight miles from the muffler shop and three miles from the precinct. The defendant's gym is located six miles from the muffler shop and four miles from the precinct. The fire station is located 100 yards from the precinct.

11. The victim was found in a white YR-15 Ford Taurus.

12. The weapon issued to police officers in Darrow County is a Smith & Wesson revolver. This type of weapon was not used in the death of Emma Jeans or in the death of Officer Morganze.

13. The murder weapon in the Emma Jeans murder was not recovered. The suicide weapon used by Officer Morganze was found at the scene. No comparison has been made between the bullets found in the Emma Jeans case and the bullet or weapon found in the Morganze case.

The following are not stipulated:

1. There is no stipulation as to the admissibility of the internal affairs investigation. If either party intends to present evidence regarding this issue, it must be raised during motions in limine.

Supplemental Police Report

THIS REPORT IS PREPARED BY OFFICER JACK BURQUETTE

CASE NUMBER YR-1-03879

My name is J. B. Burquette. I have been a detective in Darrow County for twenty-six years. Prior to being a detective, I was a uniformed officer for four years. For the last sixteen years I have been the senior investigator in the Crimes Against Persons division of the police department. I have received training in police work from the Darrow County Police, the Nita Bureau of Investigation, and the Federal Bureau of Investigation. I first learned of the homicide of Emmy Jeans by radio dispatch at approximately 10:58 p.m. on the evening of July 15, YR-1. The report was that a body had been found by a man turning in the driveway of his business, Mighty Muffler, located on North Industrial Parkway. The victim's car was found approximately 300 feet off the highway with the victim lying over the console area of her vehicle facing the passenger seat. She had clearly been shot in the head with a firearm. The owner of the business reported that since there had been heavy storms in the area earlier in the evening, he went to the muffler shop to check for any damage to his business. The owner was a white male, age sixty-five, later identified as Bill Cooper. He is not considered to be a suspect due to his answers given to police at the scene, and his alibi that he was with his spouse at the approximate time of the murder. Crime scene photos were taken, and ID was called for possible fingerprints and physical evidence gathering. The only fingerprints obtained belonged to the victim.

I was assigned by Chief Harvel to be the lead investigator. The media was notified the following morning and a request was made for any information. The body was transported for an autopsy. I was present at the autopsy along with Dr. Ingalls, chief medical examiner, and Investigator Turner who was my chief assistant. The victim was murdered with a .38 caliber Smith & Wesson weapon, by having two bullets (later identified as Remington projectiles) fired into the left side of the victim's head at close range. That range was estimated at two inches by the medical examiner. The time of death was determined to be 9:00 p.m. EST on July 15, YR-1. The autopsy was completed at 9:00 a.m. July 16, YR-1. Arrangements were made to transport the family members to the police station for questioning at 10:00 a.m.

Jerry Jeans, the victim's oldest son, was questioned first. He said he thought his younger brother had a motive to murder their mother. This was based on his belief that the younger brother was stealing money from her and that she was on to him. Jerry went on to say that she had cashed out a retirement plan six months prior to the murder that amounted to approximately $18,000.00. She was sixty-three at the time of her death and had never trusted banks. Instead, Jerry claimed, she kept all of her money in a shoe box in her closet. According to Jerry, the younger brother, Clarence, had been secretly taking cash in hopes that their mother would not count the money and discover the missing money. Jerry further stated that their mother had told him six days earlier that she had discovered $6,000.00 was missing and that he told her to call the police. He stated he was present when Officer Alex Chapman arrived to investigate the missing money. He stated that he and his mother counted out the money in the presence of Officer Chapman and indeed approximately $6,000.00 was missing. Jerry also informed Officer Chapman that Clarence had a drug problem and that the money was probably taken for drugs. Officer Chapman reportedly told Mrs. Jeans to hide the money in a safe place in her home and not to tell anyone that she had discovered the money missing. He told her and Jerry he would get a search warrant and see if he could find the missing money at Clarence's residence. Jerry further stated that on the night of the murder he got a phone call from his mother. She said she had gotten a call from Officer Chapman, and she was going to meet him to compare serial numbers on the money he had recovered and the money she still had. She did not say where she was going to meet Officer Chapman. Jerry stated that he believed that Clarence had found out about the investigation and had murdered his mother before she could meet with the police.

I did not speak to any other family members at that time. I immediately took Jerry to the victim's residence to look for the shoe box. It was not recovered at the residence. However, Jerry did identify the shoe box in question when it was located in the front passenger floor board of the vehicle we recovered from the muffler shop. I directed the other detectives to bring in Clarence Jeans for questioning. I also ordered the police report of the burglary from records. Clarence was not found immediately, but did contact police at 3:00 p.m. July 16, YR-1 to report that his mother was missing. He apparently had no television or telephone and had not been notified of his mother's murder. He was immediately questioned. He stated that he knew nothing about the missing money and did not even know his mother had cashed in her retirement. He admitted to using drugs the night of the murder and stated that he had a cocaine habit and used cocaine on a weekly basis after work. He was employed as a meat cutter at a local supermarket, but did not go to work the day after the murder. This was not uncommon according to him, and his manager was lenient with his hours because he did such a good job. He gave us permission to search his home. ID was called to photograph the home and to look for other possible evidence. No evidence was recovered.

When I returned to the station that afternoon, I found several lead sheets from citizens who had heard about the murder. Nine people had called and said they saw a police car with flashing blue lights behind the vehicle on the night of the murder. They gave different estimates on the time, but all witnesses stated they saw the officer's car and another car at the muffler shop parking lot between the hours of 8:45 and 9:27 p.m. I also found a note from the records clerk that Alex Chapman had not filed any burglary reports in the last two months. I knew we had a problem. I interviewed the witnesses personally, by telephone, regarding the police car, and had them execute witness statements by fax. Six of the eyewitnesses stated that they observed a police officer in a yellow rain jacket standing next to the driver's side of a car that was parked in front of the police car. None of the witnesses could describe the victim's vehicle except what they saw on television. All Darrow County police officers are assigned a yellow rain jacket to wear during inclement weather. The witnesses all described the police car as white with a blue stripe. This was very important because the Darrow County Police Department has six different models of police cars currently in use, each with somewhat different markings. The blue stripe is the standard making for Darrow County police vehicles. The witnesses were not mistaken.

I began to focus the investigation on Alex Chapman at 9:00 p.m. on July 16, YR-1 His police cruiser was searched without his knowledge shortly after 12:00 a.m. Officer Chapman had gotten off duty at 12:00 a.m., and the sergeant in his precinct requested he leave the car that night for service. His vehicle was searched by ID for physical evidence. The entire front seat was removed and taken by me to the crime lab at 6:00 a.m. July 17, YR-1. This was based on the autopsy finding that the perpetrator would likely have substantial blood and brain matter on his own clothing at the time of the shooting due to the close range. The crime lab technician performed the testing in my presence.

Luminol testing showed trace signs of blood residue near the arm rest. The luminol chemical can show the presence of recent human or animal blood on fibers (cotton, fabrics, and poly fibers). The test will show if blood was present in the preceding two weeks. The crime lab also detected recent cleaning chemicals present and found the underlying foam to be damp, which was indicative of a recent cleaning. Despite the luminol findings, no sufficient samples of the trace blood could be gathered by the crime lab for DNA or blood testing. However, a small blood sample was obtained that tested (O) positive, which is the same blood type as the victim. According to Chapman's personnel records, his blood type is (A) negative.

We also found an AK-47 military semi-automatic rifle in the trunk of the police car. The serial number was filed down, and the weapon was clearly illegal under Nita's Assault Weapon Ban. There was no legal reason why Officer Chapman would possess any weapon without a serial number, much less a weapon which is now banned in the State of Nita.

I had the records department gather every police radio log for the precinct on the night of the murder. No calls were made by any officer during the time of 8:45 p.m. to 9:21 p.m. This was likely due to the storms. Each officer must call in to radio dispatch if they stop or approach any vehicle during a traffic stop. This is for the officer's own safety. Also, I had Records pull all of the police reports filed by Officer Chapman in the last ten days. Although there was nothing unusual in the files, it was clear that he did not file any report in connection with the Jeans burglary. I had hoped he had labeled it under a different category such as Theft, Investigation in Progress, etc.

We also executed a search of Officer Chapman's locker at the police precinct when he came off duty at 12:00 a.m. There was no rain jacket, and the locker contained only extra ammunition and an extra police belt.

We contacted Officer Chapman at 10:00 a.m. the next morning as soon as the crime lab called with their findings of the blood sample typing. We had already issued a warrant for his arrest for one count of illegal possession of a firearm. He was asked to come to police headquarters in Nita City. He was stationed in the Northside precinct, which was approximately twenty miles from headquarters. Myself and Detective Turner were present. He was advised of the arrest warrant and advised of his *Miranda* warnings. The questioning began with the rifle. He stated he had no legal reason for the rifle, but that he had bought it after the Trayvon Martin case. He stated he was fearful about increased hostility and aggression towards police officers. He apologized for disgracing the uniform. We next began to question him about his rain jacket. He stated it was in his locker and that he had worn it on the night of the murder. He recalled that the storm was so severe that he had gone to the fire station, where he and several other officers watched television. He recalled that Officer Morganze, Officer Schmeele, and Officer Ricketts were present. They had all come to the fire station due to the rainstorm. He did not recall exactly what time he left the fire station, but he had gone to check on his business, a small gym in North Darrow County. He had run the business for several years and was an avid bodybuilder. He recalled leaving after the worst of the storm was over, but he did not recall if it was still raining hard. After he checked on his business, he returned to the fire station and watched television coverage of the storm until 11:00 p.m. There were no radio calls for his unit during that time. At 11:00 p.m. he responded a call about an accident. He got off duty at 12:00 a.m. as usual. I knew that information about the car accident call was correct because I had pulled his reports. Detective Turner radioed for the other officers to report to Headquarters for questioning. At that time, he was informed that Officer Morganze went home sick. We decided to question him the following day. We asked Chapman specifically about the murder. He denied knowing anything about it and denied stopping any vehicle. Before we could ask about the burglary, he volunteered to us that he had investigated a burglary call at the residence several days earlier and the son was a suspect. He stated that he had taken no action because the mother called him and told him she did not want to prosecute her son. He told her he would hold the report for a few days until she decided what to do. He again apologized for not following procedures. He then said something that always bothered me. He said, "The worst thing about this is that you guys think I would do a shoddy job like this. If I was going to kill somebody, I would do it better than this." He made no other comments and said he wanted to go. I asked him his locker combination. He said 5-34-23 and that the only other person who had it was Officer Morganze, because Morganze gave him the lock several years ago. During the interview, Chapman said he had no financial trouble and had recently sold some of his equipment to pay off debts. He said he got $10,000.00 cash from a wholesaler. He did not get a receipt because he did not want to claim the money on his taxes, and he could not name the buyer, stating that he did not know him. Detective Turner had checked Chapman's bank records before the interview and found that he had deposited $9,000.00 shortly after 9:00 a.m. on July 16, YR-1. Also, a detail shop called and said that Officer Chapman had brought his police cruiser in for detailing at about 10:00 a.m. July 16, YR-1. They did not see any blood on the seat, but Officer Chapman had told them to clean the seat well because he had spilled coffee on the seat the previous evening. After the interview, Officer Chapman was placed under arrest for murder and illegal possession of a firearm. He was also fired by the chief after the charges were filed. He is currently being housed without bond at the Darrow County Detention Center. He is held in an isolated cell to protect him from the other inmates. The media was notified at 3:00 p.m., and the city went crazy.

Then something unexpected happened. Officer Morganze committed suicide at 6:00 p.m. on July 17, YR-1. He finished dinner, went up to his room, and typed a suicide note on his computer saying that his daughter was not being treated fairly at school and that he could not go on. He then put his service revolver to his head and fired one shot. He was in uniform when he died. His personal life was not great and there was talk of a divorce, but the suicide came as a total shock to his wife and friends. The computer he used had been completely erased except for the suicide note. We later found the numbers "5-34-23" written on a Post-It note on his desk at the precinct.

A full internal investigation of the Northside Precinct followed, resulting in the demotion of twocaptains, three sergeants, and two watch commanders for the failure to follow police procedures. Another officer, Officer Hertz, was also arrested and indicted for the theft of $100,000.00 from the evidence room. He had checked out the money and stated he was turning it in to the FBI in Nita City. The evidence bags were found in his garage by his ex-wife. She called the police. The remainder of the internal investigation report has been sealed by court order until after the trial.

The murder charges have divided the department. Many of the officers were already aware that Chapman had been investigated in the Longhorn restaurant robbery two years ago. We did not have enough evidence to charge him, but everything pointed to an inside job. Chapman was working security, and he refused to give a polygraph after the robbery. They got away with $15,000.00 in that one night. I have no doubt that Officer Chapman killed Mrs. Jeans. The way I look at it, he murdered a grandmother in cold blood for $12,000.00. He violated the very trust that the public gave to him as a police officer. He has disgraced every officer in the department.

Whether Officer Morganze had any involvement with him we will never know, unless Officer Chapman decides to tell the truth. I do know that Officer Morganze never left the fire station that night, according to other officers present.

Ann Smith

Sworn and subscribed before me
this 19th day of September, YR-1
Notary Public

J. B. Burquette

Detective J. B. Burquette

Supplemental Police Report
Prepared For Internal Affairs

THIS REPORT IS PREPARED BY BEN TURNER

CASE NUMBER YR-1-03879

I am Detective Ben Turner, and I assisted in the investigation of the murder of Mrs. Jeans as well as the suicide of Officer Morganze. In my opinion, the two cases are related. There is no doubt that a police officer committed the murder of Mrs. Jeans. This is corroborated by several witnesses who drove by the muffler shop that night. We were never able to corroborate Alex Chapman's whereabouts on the night of the murder. He did not have an alibi at the time of the murder, but neither did Officer Morganze. The other officers who supposedly verified Morganze being at the fire station at the time of the murder were all demoted after the internal investigation. One of them was even indicted for stealing money from the police department. I don't put any credibility in their statements. They were all in trouble and were all looking out for one of their own. I guess they thought they could not help Chapman, so they hung him out to dry. The radio log for the fire station shows the firemen were called out on a possible fire right about the time of the murder. None of the firemen were able to say whether Chapman or Morganze were present on the night of the murder; only the other police officers were able to provide information about their whereabouts.

Although we asked every officer who was there to take a polygraph, every one of them refused. A few of them even got prominent defense attorneys the day they were all questioned. They know something, but they are just not talking. Chapman is just the fall guy. As far as who pulled the trigger, we will never know. Chapman claimed someone had stolen his raincoat after he learned that it was not in his locker. He also claimed that the patrolmen at the Northside precinct would often trade cars so that any number of officers might have driven his vehicle before the shooting. He said he could not remember if he was driving his own car that night. He remembered borrowing a stand-by patrol car, which we keep at the precinct. It is always parked in the first parking space and is only used about once per month if someone is having a car worked on. On the night of the murder, the stand-by car was gone for about six hours. This was confirmed by several other officers at the precinct. I even noticed it missing myself. I did not think it was that big of a deal until the witnesses began calling in saying it was a cop at the murder scene. Well, no one knows who took it because it was never formally signed out. Chapman was never one to follow procedures, and he said he never signed it out when he used it. Sure enough, he had not ever signed out that car. Even after the murder, when we were searching his car, he took the stand-by car home and did not sign it out. The stand-by car had the same blue stripes as Chapman's car. The police report in the Jeans burglary was never filed. To me, that was not unusual. Alex was a community police officer. Everyone knew him by his first name, and he would not prosecute a woman's son if she asked him not to. The missing money always bothered me when they tried to make that the motive for Chapman to murder Mrs. Jeans. I never knew Chapman to ever complain about his debts. He went about his life with the same upbeat attitude we expect from all of our officers. I never thought of him as greedy, and he would give you the shirt off his back if he though you needed it. He lived in a modest home with his wife and two children. His brother works for the sheriff's department. I would never believe that Alex Chapman would ever commit a murder. I believed him when he said he was innocent, and I still believe that today. Jack Burquette has always thought Chapman was guilty of planning an armed robbery at a restaurant where he worked security.

About two years ago, Chapman had taken a job working security at a Longhorn's restaurant on Peachtree Street. On the very first night when he was walking to his car, someone robbed the store manager who was carrying the deposits. Alex heard the yelling and ran over. He fired two shots at the perpetrator, who was described as a black male. But the perpetrator was never apprehended. Chapman was criticized for not accompanying the manager, but it was his first night. Also, the manager believed it was some kind of inside job and that Chapman had somehow been in on it. The Longhorn's had never been robbed before. Burquette worked the case and questioned Chapman for hours about his involvement. He searched Chapman's home, bank accounts, police locker, police car, everything. No evidence was ever obtained. Chapman declined to take a polygraph, saying that he did not believe in them, and that always bothered Burquette. Burquette told me several times that Chapman needed to be watched and that he could not be trusted. No charges were ever brought.

I was present during the questioning of Chapman for the murder. Burquette said that it bothered him when Chapman said, "How could you believe I would do such a shoddy murder like this?" I guess it does sound odd, but you have to know Alex. He is a perfectionist. He was saying basically, I'm not that stupid. And the truth of it is, he's not. I believe that if Chapman had wanted to do something like this, he would never be caught. He has been around enough criminals in his job to know how not to get caught. I could not believe that Burquette even questioned Chapman. It seemed like a formality. Burquette had already made his mind up, and he even brought up the Longhorn's robbery and tried to get Chapman to confess to that. I wish Burquette had waited. With more time to question the officers, we could have learned who all was involved. I do not believe for one minute that Alex Chapman ever fired that gun. He may know who did, but he did not do it. I knew Officer Morganze. He was the kind of mastermind who could dream up something like this. He and Chapman were really close. I know Chapman would have talked to Morganze about the burglary report. That is probably all Morganze needed to know. The lady had cash and a lot of it. Morganze was a computer nut who tried to keep up with the criminals on the Internet. He made back-up copies of everything. When I heard that he had erased his entire computer to write a suicide note, I knew there was a connection. I had seen him the day before the murder, and he was not acting right. He was kind of in another world. Looking back, I guess he was. When he killed himself, to me that answered the question of who killed Mrs. Jeans.

Ann Smith

Sworn and subscribed before me
this 30th day of July, YR-1.
Notary Public

Ben Turner

Detective Turner

Statement Given to Police Internal Affairs

CASE NUMBER: YR-1-03879

I UNDERSTAND THAT I AM GIVING A STATEMENT TO A LAW ENFORCEMENT OFFICER. I UNDERSTAND THAT ANYTHING I SAY MAY BE USED AGAINST ME IN COURT. I UNDERSTAND THAT I HAVE BEEN ADVISED THT I MAY HAVE AN ATTORNEY PRESENT, AND THAT I HAVE ELECTED TO HAVE MY ATTORNEY PRESENT WITH ME DURING QUESTIONING. I AM SIGNING THIS STATEMENT FREELY AND VOLUNTARILY. I UNDERSTAND AND ACKNOWLEDGE THAT THE CONTENTS OF THIS INVESTIGATION SHALL REMAIN CONFIDENTIAL AND THAT I SHALL MAKE NO MENTION OF ANY PART OF THIS INVESTIGATION EXCEPT IN A COURT OF LAW UNDER OATH. I UNDERSTAND THAT I AM NOT ENTITLED TO ANY INFORMATION ABOUT THIS INVESTIGATION FOR ANY PURPOSE.

My name is Alex Chapman. I am thirty-six years old and have never been arrested. I am a college graduate in the area of criminal justice. I was immediately hired by the Darrow County Police Department after graduation and went through the police academy. I always wanted to be in law enforcement, just like my dad and older brother. I was married at age twenty-six, and my wife and I have two children. We live near the precinct in North Darrow County. I can't believe I am sitting in jail charged with murder. It is true that I did investigate a burglary of Mrs. Jeans a couple of days before the murder. Her older son was there. I don't remember his name, but I do remember they showed me a large amount of money, which Mrs. Jeans kept in a shoe box at her trailer. They both suspected her youngest son took several thousand dollars from her. I immediately began to take notes and got an address for the younger son's residence. He apparently had drug problems and was taking the money to support his drug habit. I told her I would have to talk to my supervisor, but that we could call the son in for questioning and perhaps get his consent to search his house or possibly get a search warrant. She said she would think about it and she would call me. I could tell she was troubled. She called me at the precinct later that day. She was crying. She said her oldest son was putting a lot of pressure on her to prosecute, but that she did not want to. She knew the two sons hated each other. According to her, the oldest son said he would come over and get the rest of the money if she was not going to do anything about it. She didn't want her son arrested. She was afraid that if we went to his house, we would find drugs and then he would be locked up for a really long time. She said she wanted to think about it some more, and she begged me to please not to do anything else with the police report. I gave her my word that I would not. I know that was not the proper police procedure. We are supposed to make an incident report of everything we do, even if there is not a case. I didn't follow procedure, but I did the right thing. Being a police officer is more than procedures—it is trying to help people with their problems. I stand by what I did. Maybe I should be fired for it, but that does not mean I killed anybody.

I remember talking with Morganze about my dilemma regarding the burglary report. He agreed that nothing should be done. He asked a lot of questions about the money. I did not think it was too strange because he liked to get the details about all of my cases. It was like he was going to write a book one day, and he wanted to hear everything. That is just the way he was. He was my direct supervisor. When he said not to file a report, I listened to him. People who did not work in the Northside Precinct just did not know how things were done up there. It was a more rural part of the county. The people in our area knew us by our first names, and we knew them. We did not always follow the police protocol. That is because we did not need to follow them to do our job. It was not like we ever did anything wrong, it was just the procedures that we sometimes did not follow. I did not know any other way to police. I have only worked in the Northside Precinct, and I never cared to work anywhere else.

After the Trayvon Martin protests, I never went downtown. That is when I got the AK-47. At the time it was not illegal, and when they were outlawed in Nita, I just kept it in the trunk. I told my supervisors, and they seemed to understand my reasons. I just did not want to be attacked one day because I'm a cop and have no way to protect myself. They never told me to get rid of the gun, so I kept it in my trunk. It was always loaded in case of an emergency. Another thing about the Northside Precinct is that everyone shares their cars. It is not anything unusual for us to drive other officers' cars. That's how I know everyone knew about the rifle. I remember telling them it was in there in case they needed it. Anyway, I don't remember who all had driven my car in the two weeks prior to the murder. It was probably two or three different officers. Maybe even Morganze. I don't remember. I do remember borrowing the stand-by car on the night of the murder. It was a car that we used in case something was wrong with one of our regular cars. The keys were always kept in it, and it was parked in the very first spot at the precinct. I never signed it out, and I didn't sign it out that night. I borrowed it because my car was low on gas, and I didn't want to get wet trying to refuel my car in the rain. I parked my car at the precinct and drove the stand-by car next door to the fire station. I went in for a little while and watched television, waiting for the storm to blow over. Since the radio traffic was very light (we were not being called to go anywhere), I decided to go check on the gym. I went up there at about 9:00 p.m. I didn't keep very good watch on the exact time because I didn't know I would need to. The gym was fine, but there was a water leak. I put a trash can under the leak area and locked the place back up. I was probably in there for five or ten minutes at the most. The alarm was out so there is not even a record of me going in and out of the gym that night. After that, I drove the long way back to the fire station just in case I got a call about an accident. My route that night did not take me anywhere near the muffler shop. That is about eight miles away from my gym.

When I got back to the precinct, Morganze was not there. Almost as soon as I got back, myself and another officer responded to a near-fatal traffic accident. We worked the accident, and then I got off at my regular 12:00 a.m. time. I traded back the cars at the precinct because it had stopped raining. I filled my car up with gas and stopped to get a cup of coffee. I spilled most of it on me and the front seat, though, because my foot slipped off the brake because it was wet. I remember putting my rain jacket in my locker that night. I had it on during the car accident investigation, and I took it off after the rain stopped. I would have no reason to lie about that. Someone took my jacket from my locker. Morganze had my locker combination because he had given me the lock when I first started with the department. I don't know how any blood would have gotten on my car seat. I hurt my hand one time about six months ago when I was working an accident. I was bleeding and got some blood on the car seat at that time. But that was my blood. I did not remember my car seat being particularly damp that night when I got back in it. Of course, it was raining, and it would not have been that unusual. I did pay a detail guy to clean the car up the next day. It was so dirty because of the storm, plus the coffee stain didn't come out that well when I tried to clean it up. We have inmates who will clean the cars on the weekends, but they don't do a good job, and I think a clean car makes a good impression on the public. It is also a pride thing with me. I enjoy riding around in a clean car. I take pride in that. I paid for the car service like I always do, out of my own pocket.

It is true that I deposited $9,000.00 into my bank the day after the murder. I sold some of my gym equipment to a wholesaler who came by the gym. He paid $10,000.00 in cash. Part of the deal was that he did not give me a receipt because of the IRS laws on cash transactions. He didn't want to have to report it. That was okay with me; I didn't need a receipt. It is not unusual for me to sell and buy equipment with cash. You can get better prices that way. The gym is not very profitable and only breaks even every year. I probably won't keep it open for more than another year. People are going to bigger clubs like Gold's and Sportslife. Those gyms are really into marketing. I can't compete.

I think I paid the car detail guy $100.00 to detail the car. The other $900.00 I gave to my wife for clothes for the kids and household expenses. In terms of debts, I guess you could say I have some debts, but I wouldn't kill anybody because of it. I work an extra job doing security for high school football games and other high school events. My wife also works as a waitress on the weekends. We don't have financial problems, and we are not desperate for money.

I feel the other officers in the department know who did the murder. Everything tells me it was Morganze. Why else would he commit suicide? His alibi was no better than mine, only he had friends of his to say he was at the fire station. I know for a fact he was not there when I got back. Plus, he was the only other person I told about the money. He told me not to file the burglary report. Maybe he was planning it the whole time. When I heard about his computer being erased, I knew something was wrong. Morganze would save everything on his computer. That only goes to show that he was hiding something. Burquette had me fingered for this from the very beginning. He always thought that I had something to do with the armed robbery at the Longhorn's a few years ago. He was mad I didn't agree to a polygraph, but I don't believe in those machines. Obviously, my word as a police officer was not good enough for him. My lawyer even told me that Burquette never even investigated the family member who had known all about the money. He only looked at me because of the Longhorn's robbery. He even brought it up during the questioning. I thought after Morganze's suicide this whole case would go away and they would see who really did this. But I was wrong. My lawyers said I have to prove I'm innocent because the whole city things I'm guilty. I could have never done anything like this.

Ann Smith

Sworn and subscribed before me
this 18th day of August, YR-1
Notary Public

Alex Chapman

Alex Chapman

CRIME LAB REPORT

CASE NUMBER YR-1-03879

My name is Paul Garrison. I have been employed with the Nita Crime Lab for thirteen years. I am a lead technician and a laboratory chemist. I have been qualified as an expert in courtrooms across Nita for the last thirteen years. We do all lab work for drug testing, chemical analysis, and urine screens for law enforcement in the State of Nita.

I was asked to examine several pieces of evidence in connection with the above case number. Every piece of evidence is given a unique crime lab identification number when it is received for chain of custody purposes. I received from J. B. Burquette several items on July 16, YR-1.

ITEM NUMBER

Item 39123-95 was a car seat including arm rest.

TEST RESULTS

Car seat was first tested with luminol testing and florescent lighting. Clear indications of blood found on driver's seat and dominant coloring near arm rest. Myself and Burquette were present during testing. Burquette requested immediate DNA. However, no samples were sufficient for DNA testing were able to be obtained. I told Burquette I would gather as much residue as possible for possible blood typing. Blood typing was successful and showed 99.9 percent probability that blood type was (O) positive (same as victim). There is a margin of error due to possible chemical contaminants.

Other chemicals found in car seat: Chlorine (commonly found in bleach), water (seat was clearly damp and moist to the touch), soil solubilizing agents (2-butoxyenthanol), concentrated vinegar, surfactants, ammonia, and phosphorous. All chemical found are common household cleaning products. Also, stains apparent on foam core of seat consistent with soft drink or coffee stains.

No residual fibers were found (probably as result of recent cleaning.)

Item 39124-95 was a red stopper vial of blood labeled Emma Jeans—Autopsy.

Chemical analysis shows type (O) positive. This blood type is found in approximately fourteen percent of the human population.

Item 39125-95 was a plastic bag containing a ladies shoe box.

No fibers or fingerprints were recoverable from shoe box. No comparison possible.

Item 39126-95 was a plastic bag containing two spent Remington bullet cartridges labeled Emma Jeans—Autopsy.

Ballistics analysis shows five grooves to the left, which matches a Smith & Wesson .38 caliber revolver. All bullets have unique swirl and striation patterns. Five grooves to the right is a Remington. Five grooves to the left is a Smith & Wesson. Cannot compare to specific weapon as no gun was recovered.

Item 39127-95 was a plastic trash bag containing an AK-47 semi-automatic rifle with a scratched-out serial number and 200 bullets in a separate clip.

Microscopic analysis of the scratching on the gun does not reveal sufficient detail to accurately show serial number. Portion of letter "X" and the numbers "27" are visible. Item 39128-95 was a cut combination lock inside of a plastic bag Labeled "Chapman-Burquette."

No fingerprints could be removed from the lock in question. No comparison to any suspects is possible.

Item 39983-95 received from J. Burquette on July 19, YR-1

Item 39983-95 is a red stopper vial of blood marked "Chapman-Burquette 7-19-YR-1"

Item shows blood typing consistent with (A) positive blood. Test was successful with 99.9 percent accuracy. (A) positive blood is present in sixty-two percent of the population.

All of the above tests were completed with approved methods and procedures as provided by the Nita Department of Forensic Sciences, the Nita Bureau of Investigation, and the Nita Crime Lab. All testing was based on scientific procedures that are typically relied on by experts in the scientific community.

Ann Smith

Sworn and subscribed before me
this 30th day of July, YR-1.
Notary Public

Paul Garrison

Technician Paul Garrison

Exhibit 12

Chapman's Car

Exhibit 13

AK-47 rifle located in Chapman's vehicle trunk

Jury Charges

Indictment and Plea; Not Evidence and Plea; Not Evidence

I caution you that the fact that this accused has been indicted by the grand jury is no evidence of [*his*] guilt. You should not consider the indictment as evidence or implication of guilt, nor should the plea of not guilty to be considered as evidence.

Presumption of Innocence; Burden of Proof; Reasonable Doubt

This defendant is presumed to be innocent until proven guilty. The defendant enters the trial of the case with a presumption of innocence in [*his*] favor. This presumption remains with the defendant until it is overcome by the state with evidence sufficient to convince you beyond a reasonable doubt that the defendant is guilty of the offense charged.

No person shall be convicted of any crime unless and until each element of the crime is proved beyond a reasonable doubt.

The burden of proof rests on the state to prove every material allegation of the indictment and every essential element of the crime charged beyond a reasonable doubt.

There is no burden of proof on the defendant whatever, and the burden never shifts to the defendant to prove innocence. When a defense (except insanity) is raised by the evidence, the burden is on the state to negate or disprove it beyond a reasonable doubt.

However, the state is not required to prove the guilt of the accused beyond all doubt or to a mathematical certainty. A reasonable doubt means just what it says. It is a doubt of a fair-minded, impartial juror, honestly seeking the truth. It is a doubt based on common sense and reason. It does not mean a vague or arbitrary doubt, but is a doubt for which a reason can be given, arising from a consideration of the evidence, a lack of evidence, a conflict in the evidence, or any combination of these.

If, after giving consideration to all the facts and circumstances of this case, your minds are wavering, unsettled, or unsatisfied, then that is a doubt of the law and you should acquit the defendant; but if a doubt does not exist in your minds as to the guilt of the accused, then you would be authorized to convict the defendant.

If the state fails to prove the defendant's guilt beyond a reasonable doubt, it would be your duty to acquit the defendant.

Credibility of Witnesses

You must determine the credibility or believability of the witnesses. It is for you to determine which witness or witnesses you will believe and which witness or witnesses you will not believe, if there are some you do not believe.

In passing on their credibility, you may consider all the facts and circumstances of the case, the witnesses' manner of testifying, their intelligence, their interest or lack of interest, their means and opportunity for knowing the facts about which they testify, the nature of the facts about which they testify, the probability or improbability of their testimony, and of the occurrences about which they testify. You may also consider their personal credibility insofar as it may legitimately appear from the trial of this case.

Conflicts in Testimony

If you find a conflict when you consider the evidence in this case, you should settle this conflict, if you can, without believing that any witness made a false statement. If you cannot do this, then you should believe that witness or those witnesses you think are most entitled to belief.

You must determine what testimony you will believe and what testimony you will not believe.

Jury; Judges of Law; Facts

Members of the jury, it is my duty and responsibility to ascertain the law applicable to this case and to instruct you on that law by which you are bound. It is your responsibility to ascertain the facts of the case from all the evidence presented. It then becomes your duty and responsibility to apply the law I give you in the charge to the facts as you find them to be.

Definition of Crime

This defendant is charged with a crime against the laws of this state. A crime is a violation of a statute of this state in which there is a joint operation of an act, or omission to act, and intention.

Intent

Intent is an essential element of any crime and must be proved by the state beyond a reasonable doubt.

Intent may be shown in many ways, provided you, the jury, believe that it existed from the proven facts before you. It may be inferred from proven circumstances or by acts and conduct, or it may be, in your discretion, inferred when it is the natural and necessary consequence of the act. Whether or not you draw such an inference is a matter solely within your discretion.

No Presumption of Criminal Intent

This defendant will not be presumed to have acted with criminal intent, but you may find such intention, or the absence of it, on a consideration of words, conduct, demeanor, motive, and other circumstances connected with the act for which the accused is being prosecuted.

Transferred Intent

If one intentionally commits an unlawful act, yet the act harmed a victim other than the one intended, it is not a defense that the defendant did not intend to harm the actual person injured.

Evidence, Generally

Evidence is the means by which any fact that is put in issue is established or disproved. Evidence includes all the testimony of the witnesses and the exhibits admitted during the trial. (It also includes any facts agreed on by counsel.) It does not include the indictment or the opening statements and closing arguments made by the attorneys.

Direct and Circumstantial Evidence

Evidence may be either direct or circumstantial or both.

Direct evidence is evidence that points immediately to the question at issue.

Evidence may also be used to prove a fact by inference. This is referred to as circumstantial evidence. Circumstantial evidence is the proof of facts or circumstances by direct evidence, from which you may infer other related or connected facts that are reasonable and justified in the light of your guilt or experience.

To warrant a conviction on circumstantial evidence, the proven facts must not only be consistent with the theory of guilt, but must also exclude every other reasonable theory other than the guilt of the accused.

The comparative weight of circumstantial evidence and direct evidence, on any given issue, is a question of fact for the jury to decide.

(*Relative weight of direct and circumstantial evidence is determined by the jury where there are inconsistencies.*)

(*Where the state introduces circumstantial evidence, a charge on the law of circumstantial evidence must be given.*)

Bare Suspicion

Facts and circumstances that merely place on the defendant a grave suspicion of the crime charged, or that merely raise a speculation or conjecture of the defendant's guilt, are not sufficient to authorize a conviction of the defendant.

Alibi

The defendant contends that he was not present at the scene of the alleged offense at the time of its commission. His alibi, as a defense, involves the impossibility of the defendant's presence at the scene of the alleged offense at the time of its commission. The presence of the defendant at the scene of the crime alleged (or defendant's involvement as a co-conspirator or as a party to the crime) is an essential element of the crime set forth in this indictment, and the burden of proof rests on the state to prove such beyond a reasonable doubt.

Any evidence in the nature of the defendant's alibi should be considered by you in connection with all the other evidence in the case. If in doing so you should entertain a reasonable doubt as to the guilt of the accused, it would be your duty to acquit the defendant.

On the other hand, if you believe from the entire evidence that the defendant is guilty beyond a reasonable doubt, you may convict.

Witness, Impeached by

To impeach a witness is to prove the witness is unworthy of belief. A witness may be impeached by:

a. Disproving the facts to which the witness testified;

b. Proof of general bad character;

c. Proof that the witness has been convicted of a crime involving moral turpitude; or

d. Proof of contradictory statements, previously made by the witness as to matters relevant to the witness's testimony and to the case.

If it is sought to impeach a witness by "b," "c," or "d," above, proof of the general good character of the witness may be shown. The effect of the evidence is to be determined by the jury.

If any attempt has been made in this case to impeach any witness by proof of contradictory statements previously made, you must determine from the evidence:

First, whether any such statements were made;

Second, whether they were contradictory to any statements the witness made on the witness stand; and

Third, whether it was material to the witness's testimony and to the case.

If you find that a witness has been successfully impeached by proof of previous, contradictory statements, you may disregard that testimony unless it is corroborated by other creditable testimony, and the credit to be given to the balance of the testimony of the witness would be for you to determine.

Impeachment (Witness)

It is for you to determine whether or not a witness has been impeached and to determine the credibility of such a witness and the weight the witness's testimony shall receive in the consideration of the case.

Prior Inconsistent Statement; Substantive Evidence

Should you find that any witness, prior to the witness's testimony in this case from the witness stand, has made any statement inconsistent with that witness's testimony from the stand in this case, and that such a prior inconsistent statement is material to the case and the witness's testimony, then you are authorized to consider that prior statement not only for purposes of impeachment, but also as substantive evidence in the case.

Parties to Crime (Defined)

Every party to a crime may be charged with and convicted of commission of the crime. A person is a party to a crime only if that person:

a. Directly commits the crime;

b. Intentionally helps in the commission of the crime;

c. Intentionally advises, encourages, hires, counsels, or procures another to commit the crime; or

d. Intentionally causes some other person to commit the crime under such circumstances that the other person is not guilty of any crime either in fact or because of legal incapacity.

Principal; Failure to Prosecute; Other Involved Persons

Any party to a crime who did not directly commit the crime may be indicted, tried, convicted, and punished for commission of the crime on proof that the crime was committed and that the person was a party to it, even though the person claimed to have directly committed the crime has not been prosecuted or convicted, or has been convicted of a different crime or degree of crime, or is not amenable to justice, or has been acquitted.

Good Character of Defendant

When evidence of the good character of the defendant is offered, the jury has the duty to take that testimony, with all other evidence in the case, in determining the guilt or innocence of the defendant. Good character is a positive, substantive fact and may be sufficient to produce in the minds of a jury a reasonable doubt about the guilt of the defendant. You have the duty to take any evidence of general good character with all the other evidence in the case, and if in doing so you should entertain a reasonable doubt about the guilt of the defendant, it would be your duty to acquit. However, if you should believe the defendant guilty beyond a reasonable doubt, you would be authorized to convict, in spite of the evidence about general good character.

Malice Murder; Defined

A person commits murder when that person unlawfully and with malice aforethought, either express or implied, causes the death of another human being. Express malice is that deliberate intention to unlawfully take away the life of another human being, which is shown by external circumstances capable of proof. Malice may, but need not, be implied where no considerable provocation appears and where all the circumstances of the killing show an abandoned and malignant heart. It is for the jury to decide whether or not the facts and circumstances of this case show malice.

To constitute murder, the homicide must have been committed with malice. Legal malice is not necessarily ill will or hatred, but it is the unlawful intention to kill without justification, excuse, or mitigation.

If a killing is done with malice, no matter how short a time the malicious intent may have existed, such killing constitutes murder.

Nita law does not require premeditation, and no particular length of time is required for malice to be generated in the mind of a person. It may be formed in a moment, and instantly a mortal wound may be inflicted. Yet if malice is in the mind of the accused at the time of the doing of the act or killing, and moves the accused to do it, such is sufficient to constitute the homicide as murder.

Premeditation; Defined

(This charge should be given only if a definition of premeditation is requested by the jury.)

Premeditation, as the term is usually used, means a prior determination or plan to commit an act. Premeditation is not an element of the offense of murder and therefore need not be proven by the state to establish malice aforethought. However, any evidence of premeditation, or lack of it, may be considered by you insofar as it relates to the existence, or nonexistence, of malice at the time of the alleged killing.

Felony Murder; Defined

(Note: Felony Murder should not be charged where indictment alleges only Malice Murder, unless indictment also alleges facts showing how murder was committed sufficient to put defendant on Notice of the Underlying Felony.)

(Note: If both Malice Murder and Felony Murder are charged, you must instruct the jury to make its verdict clear as to whether they are finding the defendant "guilty of Malice Murder" or "guilty of Felony Murder.")

A person (also) commits the crime of murder when, in the commission of a felony, that person causes the death of another human being irrespective of malice. Under our law, Aggravated Assault is a felony, and is defined as follows:

Assault, Aggravated; Statutory Definitions

An assault is:

a. An attempt to commit a violent injury to the person of another; or

b. An act that places another person in reasonable apprehension of immediately receiving a violent injury. A person commits the offense of aggravated assault when that person assaults another person:

With intent to murder, rape, or rob;

With a deadly weapon, or with any object, device, or instrument that, when used offensively against a person, is likely to or actually does result in serious bodily injury.

To constitute an assault, actual injury to the other person need not be shown. It is only necessary that the evidence show, beyond a reasonable doubt, an intention to commit injury on another person, coupled with the apparent ability to commit that injury, or that the other person was intentionally placed in reasonable danger of immediately receiving a violent injury from the defendant.

The character of a weapon may be established by direct or circumstantial evidence.

Murder; Felony,

If you find and believe beyond a reasonable doubt that the defendant committed the homicide alleged in this bill of indictment at the time the defendant was engaged in the commission of the felony of Aggravated Assault, then you would be authorized to find the defendant guilty of murder, whether the homicide was intended or not. A person commits Aggravated Assault when that person assaults another person with a deadly weapon or with any object, device, or instrument that, when used offensively against a person, is likely to or actually does result in serious bodily injury. In order for a homicide to have been done in the commission of this particular felony, there must be some connection between the felony and the homicide. The homicide must have been done in carrying out the unlawful act and not collaterally to it. It is not enough that the homicide occurred sooner presently after the felony was attempted or committed. (There must be such a legal relationship between the homicide and the felony so as to cause you to find that the homicide occurred before the felony was at an end or before any attempt to avoid conviction or arrest for the felony.) The felony must have a legal relationship to the homicide, be at least concurrent with it in part, and be a part of it in an actual and material sense. A homicide is committed in the carrying out of a felony when it is committed by the accused while engaged in the performance of any act required for the full execution of the felony.

(*The following is a suggested charge to be used after charging both Malice Murder and Felony Murder.*)

If you find and believe beyond a reasonable doubt, under all the evidence and the court's instructions, that the defendant is guilty of the offense of murder with malice aforethought, then you must specify as such in your verdict, and the form of your verdict in that event would be: "We, the jury, find the defendant guilty of Malice Murder."

If you find and believe beyond a reasonable doubt, under all the evidence and the court's instructions, that the defendant is guilty of the offense of felony murder, then you must specify such in your verdict, and the form of your verdict in that event would be: "We, the jury, find the defendant guilty of Felony Murder."

Motive

Proof of particular motive is not essential to constitute the crime of murder. Evidence of motive, if any, is admitted for your determination as to whether or not it establishes the state of the defendant's mind at the time of the alleged homicide.

Corpus Delicti

The state is required to prove, beyond a reasonable doubt, that the defendant caused the death of the alleged deceased named in this bill of indictment.

If you believe from the evidence, beyond a reasonable doubt, that the defendant intentionally, unlawfully, and with malice aforethought caused the death of the alleged deceased, as in the manner alleged in this bill of indictment, then you would be authorized to find the defendant guilty.

If you believe that the death of the deceased was caused by some other act or agency with which the defendant had no connection and that the death of the alleged deceased was not caused by the defendant as in the manner alleged in this bill of indictment, or if you have any reasonable doubt as to such, then it would be your duty to acquit the defendant.

Verdict (Count 1)

If, after considering the testimony and evidence presented to you, together with the charge of the court, you should find and believe beyond a reasonable doubt that the defendant in Darrow County, Nita, did, on or about July 15, YR-1, commit the offense of Malice Murder as alleged in the indictment/accusation, you would be authorized to find the defendant guilty, and in that event, the form of your verdict would be: "We, the jury, find the defendant guilty of Malice Murder."

Verdict (Count 2)

If, after considering the testimony and evidence presented to you, together with the charge of the court, you should find and believe beyond a reasonable doubt that the defendant in Darrow County, Nita, did, on or about July 15, YR-1 commit the offense of Felony Murder as alleged in the indictment/accusation, you would be authorized to find the defendant guilty and, in that event, the form of your verdict would be: "We, the jury, find the defendant guilty of Felony Murder."

Not Guilty Verdict Form

If you do not believe that the defendant is guilty of either of these offenses, or if you have any reasonable doubt as to the defendant's guilt, then it would be your duty to acquit the defendant, in which event the form of your verdict would be: "We, the jury, find the defendant not guilty."

Unanimous Verdict

Whatever your verdict is, it must be unanimous; that is, agreed on by all. The verdict must be signed by one of your members as foreperson, dated, and returned to be published in open court.

Responsibility for Sentencing

(Note: Do not give this charge in death penalty or life without parole cases.)

You are only concerned with the guilt or innocence of the defendant. You are not to concern yourselves with punishment.

Deliberations

One of your first duties in the jury room will be to select one of your number to act as foreperson, who will preside over your deliberations and who will sign the verdict to which all twelve of you freely and voluntarily agree.

You should start your deliberations with an open mind. Consult with one another and consider each other's views. Each of you must decide this case for yourself, but you should do so after a discussion and consideration of the case with your fellow jurors. Do not hesitate to change an opinion if convinced that it is wrong. However, you should never surrender an honest opinion to be congenial or to reach a verdict solely because of the opinions of the other jurors.

Court Has No Interest in Case

By no ruling or comment the court has made during the progress of the trial has the court intended to express any opinion on the facts of this case, the credibility of the witnesses, the evidence, or the innocence of the defendant.

STATE OF NITA

STATE OF NITA	)	
	)	
	)	
	)	INDICTMENT NUMBER: CR0286
	)	
v.	)	
	)	
	)	YR-0-CR0286
	)	
ALEX CHAPMAN	)	
DEFENDANT	)	

VERDICT

COUNT 1

AS TO COUNT 1, WE THE JURY FIND THE DEFENDANT: ______________________

COUNT 2

AS TO COUNT 2, WE THE JURY FIND THE DEFENDANT: ______________________

THIS _____ DAY OF _____, YR-_____.

____

FOREPERSON

State v. Cunningham

INDICTMENT

Witnesses:

J. B. Britt
Darrow County PD

Sgt. Bill Stewart
Darrow County PD

Case No.: CR0287
Superior Court
September Term, YR-0

State of Nita

Versus

Richard Cunningham

Offense:
1. Controlled Substance Act

True BILL

Carl White
____

Carl White, Foreperson

Returned in open court by Grand Jury,

This 28th day of September, YR-0.

Barbara Underwood
____

Barbara Underwood, Clerk

The defendant herein waives a copy of indictment, list of witnesses, formal arraignment and pleads
Not guilty.

This 1st day of November, YR-0.

Richard Cunningham
____

Defendant

Lane Dixon
____

Attorney for Defendant

Elizabeth Fulton
____

Prosecutor

IN THE SUPERIOR COURT OF DARROW COUNTY
STATE OF NITA

THE GRAND JURORS selected, chosen and sworn for the County of Darrow, to wit:

1. Carl White, Foreperson
2. Helen Matthews
3. Sally Frank
4. Tim Swenson
5. Mrs. H. T. Turpin
6. Tina Epps
7. Cosmo Kramer
8. Mike Juniper
9. Larry Ferguson
10. Susan Nagel
11. Lora Colander
12. Bruce Harvey
13. Kip Stump
14. Jennifer Wyrick
15. Brad Pitt
16. Mike Mears
17. T. J. Whatley
18. Dabney Pope
19. Dianne Erickson
20. Matt Finklestein
21. Mark Henry
22. Star Shine

Count 1

in the name and behalf of the citizens of Nita, charge and accuse Richard Cunningham with the offense of Violation of the Controlled Substances Act, Nita Code § 16-5-1(a) in that the said accused, in the County of Darrow and State of Nita, on or about June 14, YR-2, did then and there unlawfully possess and distribute cocaine, a schedule II controlled substance, contrary to the laws of said state, and the good order, peace, and dignity thereof.

District Attorney
Special Presentment

Stipulations of Relevant Dates and Other Issues

The following events occurred on the following dates.

1. June 14, YR-2	The defendant arrested in Darrow County.
2. August 13, YR-2	The defendant released from jail after posting of $25,000 bond.
3. December 3, YR-2	The defendant indicted.
4. May 1, YR-1	The defendant files Motion to Reveal Identity of Confidential Informant.
5. May 20, YR-1	Order issued by Superior Court of Darrow County regarding Motion to Reveal Informant. Court finds that the informant is neither a witness nor a participant and therefore merely a tipster. Motion is therefore denied.
6. June 11, YR-1	The defendant makes written complaint to Internal Affairs.
7. June 18, YR-1	Internal Affairs takes written statements from parties.
8. June 19, YR-1	Internal Affairs seals records. Makes no findings of wrongdoing.
9. November 20, YR-1	First trial of the defendant, ends in mistrial with deadlocked jury.

The following facts are stipulated by the parties.

1. The substance obtained from Cunningham tested positive for cocaine at the state crime lab. No objections will be made to the crime lab report.
2. There is no dispute as to chain of custody of the cocaine. No objections will be heard regarding chain of custody.
3. There are no audio or video recordings of this case.
4. The defendant must be male. Detective Britt must be male. At trial, the state/civil defendants must call Detective J. B. Britt and Sgt. Bill Stewart; the defense/civil plaintiffs must call Richard Cunningham and Roty Williams.
5. The Hi Restaurant in question is located in Darrow County.
6. The defendant was properly Mirandized by the officers at the time of arrest.

7. Jerry Peterson and Theresa Kincaid are unavailable witnesses under Federal Rule of Evidence 804(b)(5)/Nita hearsay exemptions. The witnesses cannot be located for trial.

8. All documents included as part of problem materials are certified copies, if applicable.

The following are not stipulated.

1. There is no stipulation as to the admissibility of the internal affairs investigation or finding. If either party intends to present evidence regarding this issue, it must be raised during motions in limine.

2. There is not a stipulation as to the admissibility of the following:

    a. initial police report

    b. final police report

    c. warrant application

    d. warrant for arrest

    e. notes taken by arresting officer

    f. property sheet

Supplemental Police Report

PREPARED FOR INTERNAL AFFAIRS

CASE NUMBER: 0039-YR-2

My name is J. B. Britt. I am an officer with the City of Nita. I have been in law enforcement for four years. For my first three years, I worked as a patrol officer. I was later assigned to the Multi-Jurisdictional Drug Task Force with the Darrow County Police Department. The task force gets federal funding to target illegal drug trade and consists of twelve officers who are all loaned from other departments to the Task Force. I was trained by the other members of the task force in undercover work and surveillance for three months. Then I started making my own cases. The case involving Richard Cunningham was one of the first cases I worked myself. I was supervised during the entire investigation of Mr. Cunningham by other officers within the task force.

I first met Cunningham through some information I received from an informant named Theresa Kincaid. She had been arrested by another task force officer for the sale of three grams of methamphetamine in March YR-2. She worked at the Hi Restaurant before her arrest and told us she could help in the prosecution of other drug suspects who she routinely came into contact with at her job. We arranged for her to be released on a low bond from the county jail, and she went back to work at the Hi Restaurant, only this time she was also working for us. We got a call from her about two weeks after she got out of jail. My records show it was May 20, YR-2. She stated that she had come into contact with a customer who stated he could supply her with a quantity of cocaine. I told her to give the suspect my cell phone number and to tell him my name was J. B.

My records indicated I spoke with Cunningham at least ten times. I keep track of my phone calls on a piece of paper with the time I called the suspect. Apparently, the paper was misfiled because I have recently just located it for this hearing out of another file. The first call was when I called Cunningham on May 22, YR-2, at approximately 2:30 p.m. He stated his name was Richard and told me his address was 310 Lodge Apartments. I knew right away he was lying because the Lodge Apartments are a single story and not three stories tall. Thus, there would not be a "310" room number. I did know the Lodge Apartments are located in a known drug area. He stated he could obtain cocaine for me. I asked him if he could get powder cocaine as well as crack. Cunningham stated that he could get me crack, powder, or an eight ball. He quoted me prices on each and stated that he would get the cocaine from a source of his who was staying at a local hotel. Cunningham stated that he did not have a car and that if I wanted the cocaine that night, he would need me to give him a ride to the hotel. Because the hotel was located in another county outside my jurisdiction, I did not take Cunningham up on his offer. We are not allowed to arrest suspects in other counties. I told him to call me when he got some cocaine he could sell me. He said he would and hung up. Before he hung up, I gave him the number to the place I work at night. I do not specifically recall how many times Mr. Cunningham called me during this investigation, although I was called several times by the informant. All of this information should be in my notes.

I did not hear from him right away. I contacted the informant and asked what had happened. She stated she would get back to me. Later that night, on June, 1, YR-2, Cunningham called and said he still did not have any cocaine. Since he lived in Darrow County, I drove to Cunningham's apartment to see if he was telling me the truth. He had previously told Theresa he lived in apartment number 310. When I arrived, there was no 310, as I suspected. Therefore, I assumed he was located in Room 103. I was equipped with a wireless body bug, and my conversations were monitored by four other officers in the parking lot. We always do this for safety reasons. If he had sold me drugs, we would have additional officers to help with the arrest. I knocked on the door, and Cunningham answered. I told him who I was. He was somewhat surprised to see me, but I told him I was really needing some cocaine and asked him to make some calls to see if I could score me some. I acted the part of an addict desperate for drugs. He bought it and made several calls, stating he was calling some of his suppliers. I stayed for about an hour and a half and watched a baseball game with Cunningham. Before I left, I asked Cunningham if he didn't have any private stash he could sell me. He got all uptight and said that he didn't use drugs. I told him he was overreacting. He got a strange look on his face and asked me if I was a cop. I told him I was beginning to think the same thing about him. That seemed to calm him down. This is the same answer we are trained to give in such situations.

Again, I didn't hear anything from him right away. After a few days, I called the informant and asked what was going on. Cunningham called me that night and said he thought he could get something. I told him to call me when he had it. It was June 10, YR-2. I waited until midnight and called him. I told him I was tired of him jerking me around and wanted to know whether he was going to come through for me. Again, I was playing the part of a desperate drug addict. He said he was sorry and said he would call me the next day. He didn't. Instead, the informant later called and said she had talked to Cunningham and he had the stuff. She said she would go to his apartment to make sure he was not lying. Once the informant verified that she actually had seen Cunningham with cocaine, I arranged the informant to meet with Cunningham behind the Hi Restaurant after work. She got off work at 6:00 p.m. Cunningham was to meet her the next day, June 14, YR-2.

We had a team of officers present. Cunningham approached the informant behind the Hi Restaurant, and she directed him to my vehicle. It was wired and being monitored by the other officers. Cunningham asked me if I could give him a ride home. I told him to let me see the stuff. He pulled it out of his pants. He was eating a Subway sandwich while he tried to talk to me. He was mumbling and said it was good stuff and handed me a small plastic baggie containing suspected powder cocaine. I gave the money to Cunningham. It was $300.00 for what appeared to be four grams. Cunningham then said something to the effect that this was the same stuff he had given the informant and that she liked it. I do not know what he meant by this statement. Then everything happened real fast. Cunningham appeared to be trying to flee. Theresa was right behind Cunningham and tripped him or something. Cunningham was on the ground and complaining about an injury to his eye. Apparently, Cunningham fell on a rock in the parking lot. Cunningham was asked to make a statement after his arrest, but he opted to talk with an attorney before speaking with us. We did not seek a search warrant based on there being no drugs in the residence on the prior occasion when I visited the suspect. The defendant had no other drugs, weapons, or money on his person at the time of the arrest. There were no visible signs of drug use.

He was taken to the county jail, and a warrant was obtained for his arrest on the charge of sale of cocaine. He was not given a bond by the magistrate judge due to the nature of the charge. The informant was given the normal and customary fees paid in such cases, $250. She was also used in connection with other cases. Due to her cooperation with our investigation, we have recommended to the district attorney that her charges be dropped. No other cases in which she has offered information have gone to trial. As part of our deal, she is required to testify in the prosecution of any cases for which she is responsible for providing leads. However, if the court does not require the informant to testify, they are not required to be in court.

It is customary to record all phone calls with suspects. However, this was not done in this case since Cunningham never had any drugs when we spoke on the phone. There may have been other phone calls to Cunningham that I did not make any note of. I would not have made any notation of a call unless Cunningham had drugs to sell. If he did not have anything, I would likely not make a note of it. If the informant called more frequently to talk to Cunningham, I have never been told that.

There is no doubt that Cunningham sold me the drugs that night. He is a drug dealer. I offered Cunningham the same deal as I offered Theresa. Everybody gets the chance to help themselves. Cunningham refused to say anything except that he had gotten the drugs from some hotel and didn't know anyone who sold drugs.

Ann Smith

Sworn and subscribed before me
this 18th day of June, YR-1
Notary Public

J.B. Brit

Detective J. B. Britt

Supplemental Police Report

PREPARED FOR INTERNAL AFFAIRS

CASE: 0039-YR-2

My name is Sgt. Bill Stewart. I have been a sworn police officer for the last nine years and have worked as a Sergeant for the last six years with the Drug Task Force. I am in charge of the Drug Task Force and the supervision of the training of new officers for the Drug Task Force. I did not personally train J. B. Britt. All undercover officers are taught to record all phone conversations with potential suspects. This is done for two reasons. First, it acts as a record in the event there is a later problem in the case. Second, the recordings can rebut any claim of entrapment by the suspects. We often use confidential informants in undercover drug operations. Often, informants can offer information and end up working off their own criminal charges. Of course, the ultimate decision is made by the District Attorney. It is important that informants do not compromise an investigation. If it were learned that an informant was using drugs or engaging in other illegal conduct, the entire case would be jeopardized. I would not participate in a case under such circumstances. If the informant is not honest with the undercover officer, this might also jeopardize an operation.

I am familiar with the case against Cunningham. I was briefed on the case shortly before the arrest of Cunningham by J. B. Britt. Britt told me and the other members of the Drug Task Force that we would be doing a takedown on Cunningham at the Hi Restaurant. He stated that he had been in contact with Cunningham for several weeks and was given his name by an informant who was a waitress at the Hi Restaurant. I do not recall her name, and the name is not in the report of the incident. She indicated that Cunningham might be a major player, always coming into the Hi Restaurant flashing large amounts of money and bragging that he could get the girls drugs if they would go out with him. According to her, he would come into the Hi Restaurant every night. Cunningham had been reluctant to do a drug transaction in Darrow County, although an attempted buy had already been set up at his apartment. When the undercover officer arrived, Cunningham said he had no drugs and appeared very nervous. Britt had thought that Cunningham might have been on to his cover. At the Hi Restaurant, we were to wait in other undercover vehicles while Britt made the purchase of cocaine in his pickup truck. The truck was wired for sound, and once the takedown signal was given, we would move in and make the arrest. We arrested the suspect and collected several bags of suspected cocaine from him. Detective Britt later tested the substance at the Drug Annex with the use of a NIK test. It tested positive for cocaine. In undercover work, a lot of an officer's time is spent on the phone making contact with drug dealers and letting them know he is ready to do business. Officers are not allowed to solicit sales and can only ask if the suspect has any drugs to sell. Officers are normally allowed to work on their own. We don't clock in or out. We work our leads and develop a relationship with the dealers. Often times, we have to assume an identity and place ourselves in the criminal underworld. Sometimes we have to go to their homes, other times we meet at bars or other locations. Generally, we meet the dealers wherever we can. Britt had informed us that for this particular operation he had assumed the identity of an addict. He said he had Cunningham convinced that he was addicted to drugs and was also a dealer himself. I was present the night Cunningham was arrested. We read him his *Miranda* rights, and he elected to talk to his attorney. We told him that he was not doing himself any favors by not cooperating and not working with us as an informant. I guess he thought he knew what he was doing.

I have never been accused of entrapment. In most of my cases, we are able to turn the smaller dealers into informants and eventually try to make cases on the larger dealers. On the night of his arrest, Cunningham said nothing about wanting to work with us. To me, he could have done himself a big favor, but he chose not to cooperate. That was his choice. I have reviewed the case with J. B. Britt after the allegations of entrapment came up at an earlier hearing to reveal the confidential informant. The judge didn't buy it. I found no evidence of entrapment in my review of the case.

Ann Smith

Sworn to and subscribed before me
this 18th day of June, YR-1
Notary Public

Bill Stewart

Detective Sgt. Bill Stewart

Statement Given to Police Internal Affairs

CASE NUMBER: 0039-YR-2

I, UNDERSTAND THAT I AM GIVING A STATEMENT TO A LAW ENFORCEMENT OFFICER. I UNDERSTAND THAT ANYTHING I SAY MAY BE USED AGAINST ME IN COURT. I UNDERSTAND THAT I HAVE BEEN ADVISED THAT I MAY HAVE AN ATTORNEY PRESENT AND THAT I HAVE ELECTED TO HAVE MY ATTORNEY PRESENT WITH ME DURING QUESTIONING. I AM SIGNING THIS STATEMENT FREELY AND VOLUNTARILY. I UNDERSTAND AND ACKNOWLEDGE THAT THE CONTENTS OF THIS INVESTIGATION SHALL REMAIN CONFIDENTIAL AND THAT I SHALL MAKE NO MENTION OF ANY PART OF THIS INVESTIGATION EXCEPT IN A COURT OF LAW UNDER OATH. I UNDERSTAND THAT I AM NOT ENTITLED TO ANY INFORMATION ABOUT THIS INVESTIGATION FOR ANY PURPOSE.

My name is Richard Cunningham. I am twenty-eight years old and have never been arrested. I am a college graduate and work in telemarketing for a regional electronics distributor in Nita. The company is Petrus Electronics. I have been there for three years, ever since I graduated from college. I never thought I would find myself in this situation. Since I am from New York, I couldn't even get anyone to make my bond for me, and I ended up spending fifty-eight days in jail before I could get my parents to get me a local attorney to get a bond set for me. By the time I was released, I had lost my job, and all my furniture and personal belongings were gone. My apartment company put everything on the side of the road when I didn't pay the rent that month.

This experience has really made me realize how stupid I was to get involved with this guy named J. B. I always thought something was funny about him, but I assumed it was his drug addiction. He was always calling me and pestering me about drugs. Apparently, I had made some offhand comment to a waitress at the Hi Restaurant while I was eating dinner there one night. I had thought she was attractive since I met her. Her name was Theresa Kincaid. Although I was always trying to flirt with her, she never really paid any attention to me. On that night, though, she really started staring at me and smiling. I asked her what she was doing looking at me like that. She said she thought I had real cute, pretty eyes and that she wanted to see me after she got off work. I waited around until she got off work at 9:00 p.m. She came and sat down next to me in the booth. She said something about wanting to get together that night. I told her sure. Then she said she wanted to know if I could get her some blow. I had been to parties and had seen people use cocaine before, although I myself have never used cocaine. But I knew she was talking about drugs. I said sure, meaning that if she wanted to get some, I knew where she could go. She said she did not want to go out unless I had some blow and said that she couldn't afford to buy it on her tips from the Hi Restaurant. I guess she wanted me to buy it for her, and then we could go out. I told her that I did not have a car and couldn't. She kind of acted like she had changed her mind about going out. I tried to ask her if she still wanted to go out after work with her driving, but she acted like she wasn't interested. I began to thing at that point that she was addicted to drugs. She just was not acting normal, you know, with the mood swings. I caught a ride from a friend home that night. She had given me her number and said she may call sometime. I think I also gave her my cell number and home number that night.

It was not too long later that that I first heard from a guy named J. B. He called and said he was a friend of Theresa's from the Hi Restaurant. I didn't know what he was talking about at first, but he got right to the point. He said Theresa had told him that I had cocaine for sale. I told him like I told her, but she had apparently told him that I had cocaine in my apartment all the time. I told him I don't use drugs and that I didn't have any drugs. He said he wanted to know where I lived in case I was able to get any drugs. It was kind of like he didn't want to drive too far out of his way and that he had other suppliers who were closer. I was sitting around that night watching a baseball game at my apartment. My roommate, Jerry, was there for a little while, but I think he had left to go out.

The next thing I knew, this guy J. B. was at my door. I opened up the door, and he looked all strung out on drugs. He said he really needed some cocaine and asked to come in. I didn't think I had much choice. I let him inside, and he began to plead with me to get him some drugs. I didn't know what to do. I called Theresa first, but she was not home. Next, I acted like I was calling people so he would think I was trying to help. I then talked to him and told him I was sorry, but that I didn't have any drugs and that I didn't do that kind of thing. I told him I had dated girls who had used drugs, but that I didn't make a habit out of obtaining drugs for people like he evidently assumed. He said he would wait for my suppliers to call me back. I acted like I was calling people again. I then told him I didn't have any suppliers, but that these people I had called might know somebody. I told him if he was really desperate, he needed to go downtown or to one of the hotels where they sell it on the street. He said he couldn't do that because he had been busted before and that if he got caught again he would face jail time. I tried to change the subject to the baseball game, which we watched, but he kept wanted to talk about drugs. I finally began to think he was acting very strange. I can't explain it, but I thought it was the fact that he was on drugs. After about an hour and a half, he said that I should just sell him some of my own stash. I said, "What's wrong with you? You think I would sit here all night and act like I don't have anything so that I can sell you some after waiting for an hour?" Then I said to him that he sure was acting strange showing up like this and then asking a question like that, and that I thought he was the police. He got off the sofa and got right in my face. I have never been so scared. He got about an inch away from my face and said he was beginning to think I was the police! He then said for me not to jerk him around again and that I had better be calling.

I told Theresa what happened later that night. She told me not to worry and that he was just weird. She also said she was sorry she ever told him to call, but that she thought I was a drug dealer and could get him what he wanted. I told her to please call and tell him that I could not help him. I also told my roommate what happened. He said to let him know if J. B. called again and that we could call the police and have him arrested. I didn't want to get Jerry involved, especially with J. B. getting in my face. We both began to worry though about what J. B. might do if he really thought I was the police and that he might go back to jail.

I thought that I had solved the problem by talking to Theresa. But sure enough, J. B. started calling me two or three times a day. I would not return his calls. I had given him my number when he was over at the house. One day, though, he called me at home and asked why I was jerking him around and why I was not returning his calls. He was yelling and was very angry. He said he going to assume I was a police officer unless I got him drugs within forty-eight hours. Then he hung up. I called Theresa, but she wouldn't call me back. My roommate was not home. I went next door to Roty's apartment. I told Roty the situation. Roty knew some people who had sold drugs before and tried to call them. I told Roty I was scared, and Roty said I should be. Roty knew a guy who was an informant who ended up getting shot by a dealer four weeks earlier. Roty knew I didn't have a car and suggested we go to one of the street corners in downtown Nita City and buy J. B. some drugs. That way, Roty said, J. B. would know I was not a cop, and even though I would never sell him drugs again, he would know I was not an informant. It seemed to make sense, and I was panicking. We got in the car and drove toward downtown Nita City. On the way, we drove by a motel with people hanging around in the parking lot. I told Roty to turn around and drive through to see if anyone had anything. Roty had all the money and immediately upon pulling into the parking lot, two people walked up and asked him what he needed. Roty said $300.00 worth of powder. One of the guys went into a room and within thirty seconds the drugs were under Roty's seat, and we were driving out of the lot. The hotel was the Royal Inn off of Piedmont Road in Nita City, Darrow County.

I called Theresa and told her to come pick up the stuff at my apartment. She said she would the next day. She showed up and asked for the drugs. I gave the stuff to her and told her to pay me $300.00, which was what me and Roty had paid. She took out some of the powder on her small fingernail and snorted it right there in my apartment. She smiled and handed me back the drugs. She said not to tell J. B. that she had sampled the merchandise and that she couldn't take the drugs because J. B. did not give her any money. I told her she could owe me and to just take the drugs, but she refused. Roty was not there when this happened, but was there when she came out of my apartment afterward. She didn't say anything to him and just left. I told Roty what happened. Roty said I should take the drugs to them and make sure to do the deal in a public place so J. B. wouldn't try to rob me. Theresa had said that J. B. would come to the Hi Restaurant later on that night. I made arrangements to get a ride to work, and I kept the cocaine in my underwear during my shift. After work, I went to Hi Restaurant. I wanted to give the drugs to Theresa inside, but she told me J. B. was outside with the money.

When I got to the pickup truck J. B. was in, I asked him for a ride home, and he said he would give me one. Then, even though Theresa had told me not to, I told J. B. that Theresa had tried the stuff earlier and that she liked it. He acted as if he didn't hear me, but I didn't want him to think I was trying to rip him off, and I wanted him to know that he could trust me to tell him the truth, especially about not being a cop. The next thing I knew, the police were everywhere, only I didn't know they were police officers. They were wearing masks and yelling, "Get your hands down." They threw me on the ground and started pushing me into the ground. I was so scared. I thought I was going to be robbed. I couldn't believe they were the police. I had been set up by them all along. I just want to know, why me? Why did they keep after me like that?

Ann Smith	*Richard Cunningham*
Sworn and subscribed before me this 18th day of June, YR-1 Notary Public	Richard Cunningham

Statement Given to Police Internal Affairs

CASE NUMBER: 0039-YR-2

I UNDERSTAND THAT I AM GIVING A STATEMENT TO A LAW ENFORCEMENT OFFICER. I UNDERSTAND THAT ANYTHING I SAY MAY BE USED AGAINST ME IN COURT. I UNDERSTAND THAT I HAVE BEEN ADVISED THAT I MAY HAVE AN ATTORNEY PRESENT AND THAT I HAVE ELECTED TO HAVE MY ATTORNEY PRESENT WITH ME DURING QUESTIONING. I AM SIGNING THIS STATEMENT FREELY AND VOLUNTARILY. I UNDERSTAND AND ACKNOWLEDGE THAT THE CONTENTS OF THIS INVESTIGATION SHALL REMAIN CONFIDENTIAL AND THAT I SHALL MAKE NO MENTION OF ANY PART OF THIS INVESTIGATION EXCEPT IN A COURT OF LAW UNDER OATH. I UNDERSTAND THAT I AM NOT ENTITLED TO ANY INFORMATION ABOUT THIS INVESTIGATION FOR ANY PURPOSE.

My name is Roty Williams, and I am twenty-six years old. I work as a bartender at a local hotel. I would rather not say the location. My name is pronounced ROT-ee. At the time of his arrest, I had known Richard for fourteen months, since I moved in next door to him at the complex. I can certainly vouch for his good character. He is always very friendly and considerate. He will lend me money if I need to pay a bill, and he will take me out to eat with him a lot. Richard has not had a car since I have known him. He always says he is saving up for a Mercedes, but I think he is just frugal with his money and doesn't think he needs one. He does not live a lavish lifestyle and has very few furnishings. I know he used to work two jobs and not come home until late sometimes. I don't remember seeing the person Richard told me about known as J. B. come to the apartment. But I thought I remembered a guy who looked similar to him sitting in a car one day outside of our building. He wasn't doing anything but sitting there. It was about one week before Richard was arrested. I have been shown a photograph of Detective J. B. Britt by Internal Affairs. He looks like the man I saw in the parking lot that day. I would recognize him in court.

I don't really know too much about Richard. One night, though, he came running over in a panic. He said he had gotten involved with some waitress and that she had told a friend of hers that Richard was a cocaine supplier. The guy's name was J. B., and he had showed up at Richard's apartment earlier that night. Richard said J. B. wanted drugs because he was an addict. But what seemed to frighten him the most was that J. B. thought he was the police because he never had any drugs to sell. I told him a friend of mine had recently been shot in Nita City by a dealer who mistakenly though he was a cop. That seemed to upset him more. I told him I would make some calls to see if any of the people I know could get some cocaine to sell to J. B. No one called back. I told Richard if he was smart, he would get that guy some drugs so that he would know he was not a narc. Then the guy wouldn't bother him anymore about being a narc, and he would only have to do this one time and it would all be over. I kind of feel responsible for all that happed to Richard. I remember when the landlord evicted him and Jerry because Jerry couldn't pay the rent without Richard. I haven't seen Jerry since.

The night I helped him get the drugs was weird. We were on our way to downtown Nita City to buy some cocaine. We drove by a motel, and Richard said that it looked like a drug place because there was a group of people hanging out in the parking lot. I think it was the Royal Inn. I don't remember the street it was on. We bought four bags of powder from one of the guys standing in the parking lot. I put them right under my seat and drove away. I was sure scared. When we got back to the apartment, Richard said thanks and went inside. He seemed relieved that he could get this guy J. B. off his back. The next day I saw Theresa Kincaid leave Richard's apartment. Richard didn't say anything at that point, but he told me later who it was. He said later that J. B. wanted him to meet at the Hi Restaurant. I told him to get rid of that stuff and not to get hurt. The next day Jerry came by and told me Richard was arrested. I couldn't believe it. I thought for sure the police were also going to come and get me, but they never even called. Richard told me to be here today, and I am telling whole truth. I know that I may face charges for my involvement, but I have to tell the truth about this incident. I have talked to Richard and his lawyer before coming here today. I have even had to hire a lawyer to be with me here today. I know I am in big trouble.

Ann Smith

Sworn and subscribed before me
this 18th day of June, YR-1
Notary Public

Roty Williams

Roty Williams

Exhibit 14

Cocaine delivered by Cunningham

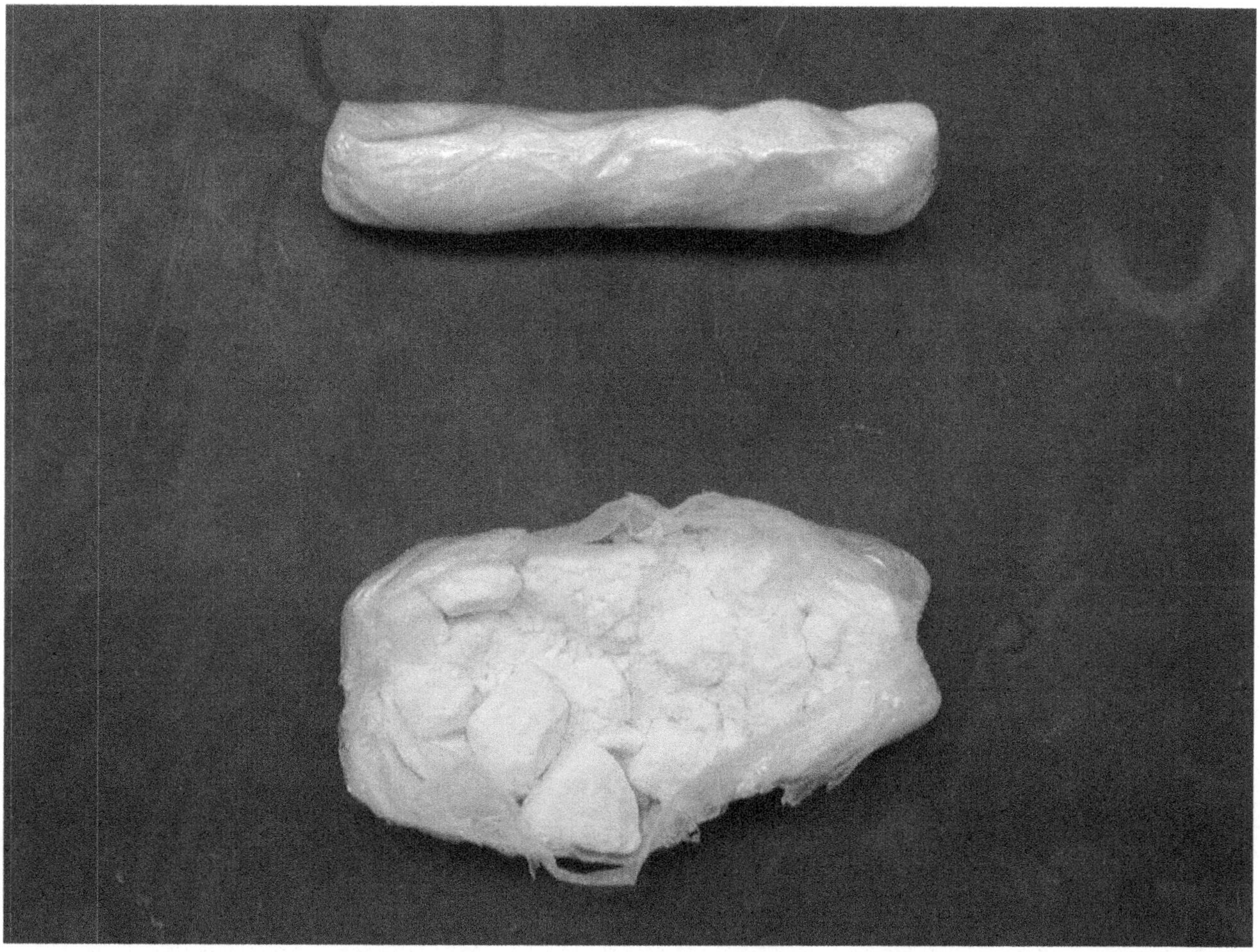

Exhibit 15

Royal Inn

Exhibit 16

Room 103 (on left), Room 104 (on right)

Exhibit 17

Hi Restaurant

JURY CHARGES

Indictment and Plea; Not Evidence and Plea; Not Evidence

I caution you that the fact that this accused has been indicted by the grand jury is no evidence of his guilt. You should not consider the indictment as evidence or implication of guilt, nor should you consider a plea of not guilty as evidence.

Presumption of Innocence; Burden of Proof; Reasonable Doubt

This defendant is presumed to be innocent until proven guilty. The defendant enters on the trial of the case with a presumption of innocence in his favor. This presumption remains with the defendant until it is overcome by the state with evidence that is sufficient to convince you beyond a reasonable doubt that the defendant is guilty of the offense charged.

No person shall be convicted of any crime unless and until each element of the crime is proved beyond a reasonable doubt.

The burden of proof rests on the state to prove every material allegation of the indictment and every essential element of the crime charged beyond a reasonable doubt.

There is no burden of proof on the defendant whatever, and the burden never shifts to the defendant to prove innocence. When a defense (except insanity) is raised by the evidence, the burden is on the state to negate or disprove it beyond a reasonable doubt.

However, the state is not required to prove the guilt of the accused beyond all doubt or to a mathematical certainty. A reasonable doubt means just what it says. It is a doubt of a fair-minded, impartial juror, honestly seeking the truth. It is a doubt based on common sense and reason. It does not mean a vague or arbitrary doubt, but is a doubt for which a reason can be given, arising from a consideration of the evidence, a lack of evidence, a conflict in the evidence, or any combination of these.

If, after giving consideration to all the facts and circumstances of this case, your minds are wavering, unsettled, or unsatisfied, then that is a doubt of the law, and you should acquit the defendant. If doubt does not exist in your minds as to the guilt of the accused, then you would be authorized to convict the defendant.

If the state fails to prove the defendant's guilt beyond a reasonable doubt, it would be your duty to acquit the defendant.

Credibility of Witnesses

You must determine the credibility or believability of the witnesses. It is for you to determine which witness or witnesses you will believe and which witness or witnesses you will not believe, if there are some you do not believe.

In determining their credibility, you may consider all the facts and circumstances of the case, the witnesses' manner of testifying, their intelligence, their interest or lack of interest, their means and opportunity for knowing the facts about which they testify, the nature of the facts about which they testify, the probability or improbability of their testimony, and of the occurrences about which they testify. You may also consider their personal credibility insofar as it may legitimately appear from the trial of this case.

Conflicts in Testimony

If you find a conflict when you consider the evidence in this case, you should settle this conflict, if you can, without believing that any witness made a false statement. If you cannot do this, then you should believe that witness or those witnesses you think are most entitled to belief.

You must determine what testimony you will believe and what testimony you will not believe.

Jury; Judges of Law; Facts

Members of the jury, it is my duty and responsibility to ascertain the law applicable to this case and to instruct you on that law by which you are bound. It is your responsibility to ascertain the facts of the case from all the evidence presented. It then becomes your duty and responsibility to apply the law I give you in the charge to the facts as you find them to be.

Definition of Crime

This defendant is charged with a crime against the laws of this state. A crime is a violation of a statute of this state in which there is a joint operation of an act, or omission to act, and intention (*or criminal negligence*).

Intent

Intent is an essential element of any crime and must be proved by the state, beyond a reasonable doubt.

Intent may be shown in many ways, provided you, the jury, believe that it existed from the proven facts before you. It may be inferred from the proven circumstances or by acts and conduct, or it may be, in your discretion, inferred when it is the natural and necessary consequence of the act. Whether or not you draw such an inference is a matter that lies solely within your discretion.

(*Use the following charge with caution in cases involving "specific intent."*)

Criminal intent does not mean an intention to violate the law or to violate a penal statute, but means simply to intend to commit an act that is prohibited by a statute.

No Presumption of Criminal Intent

This defendant will not be presumed to have acted with criminal intent, but you may find such intention, or the absence of it, on a consideration of words, conduct, demeanor, motive, and other circumstances connected with the act for which the accused is being prosecuted.

Transferred Intent

If one intentionally commits an unlawful act, yet the act harmed a victim other than the one intended, it is not a defense that the defendant did not intend to harm the actual person injured.

Evidence, Generally

Evidence is the means by which any fact that is put into issue is established or disproved. Evidence includes all the testimony of the witnesses and the exhibits admitted during the trial. (*It also includes any facts agreed to by counsel.*) It does not include the indictment or the opening statements and closing arguments made by the attorneys.

Direct and Circumstantial Evidence

Evidence may be either direct or circumstantial or both.

Direct evidence is evidence that points immediately to the question at issue.

Evidence may also be used to prove a fact by inference. This is referred to as circumstantial evidence. Circumstantial evidence is the proof of facts or circumstances, by direct evidence, from which you may infer other related or connected facts that are reasonable and justified in light of your experience.

To warrant a conviction on circumstantial evidence, the proven facts must not only be consistent with the theory of guilt, but must also exclude every other reasonable theory other than the guilt of the accused.

The comparative weight of circumstantial evidence and direct evidence, on any given issue, is a question of fact for the jury to decide.

(*Relative weight of direct and circumstantial evidence is determined by the jury where there are inconsistencies.*)

(*Where state introduces circumstantial evidence, a charge on the law of circumstantial evidence must be given.*)

Bare Suspicion

Facts and circumstances, which merely place on the defendant a grave suspicion of the crime charged, or which merely raise a speculation or conjecture of the defendant's guilt, are not sufficient to authorize a conviction of the defendant.

Entrapment

The defendant contends that he was entrapped by law enforcement officers or their agents to commit the offense charged. Entrapment is an affirmative defense that must be proved by the defendant with evidence that is sufficient to convince you that he was in fact entrapped by officers or their agents. In the event that entrapment has been proven to your satisfaction, the burden then shifts to the state to disprove the elements of entrapment beyond a reasonable doubt.

Entrapment exists where the idea to commit the criminal act for which the defendant is being charged (a) originated with officers of the state or their agents, and (b) but for the intervention of the state actors, the crime would not have been committed.

Any evidence in the nature of entrapment should be considered by you in connection with all the other evidence in the case. If, in doing so, you should entertain a reasonable doubt as to the guilt of the accused, it would be your duty to acquit the defendant. On the other hand, if you believe from the entire evidence that the defendant is guilty beyond a reasonable doubt, you may convict.

Witness, Impeached by

To impeach a witness is to prove the witness is unworthy of belief. A witness may be impeached by:

a. Disproving the facts to which the witness testified;

b. Proof of general bad character;

c. Proof that the witness has been convicted of a crime involving moral turpitude; or

d. Proof of contradictory statements, previously made by the witness, as to matters relevant to the witness's testimony and to the case.

If it is sought to impeach a witness by "b," "c," or "d," above, proof of the general good character of the witness may be shown. The effect of the evidence is to be determined by the jury.

If any attempt has been made in this case to impeach any witness by proof of contradictory statements previously made, you must determine from the evidence:

a. First, whether any such statements were made;

b. Second, whether such statements were contradictory to any statements the witness made on the witness stand; and

c. Third, whether the statements were material to the witness's testimony and to the case.

If you find that a witness has been successfully impeached by proof of previous contradictory statements, you may disregard that testimony unless it is corroborated by other creditable testimony, and the credit to be given to the balance of the testimony of the witness would be for you to determine.

Impeachment (Witness)

It is for you to determine whether or not a witness has been impeached and to determine the credibility of such a witness and the weight the witness's testimony shall receive in the consideration of the case.

Prior Inconsistent Statement; Substantive Evidence

Should you find that any witness, prior to their testimony in this case from the witness stand, has made any statement inconsistent with that witness's testimony from the stand in this case, and that such prior inconsistent statement is material to the case and the witness's testimony, then you are authorized to consider that prior statement not only for purposes of impeachment, but also as substantive evidence in the case.

Parties to Crime (Defined)

Every party to a crime may be charged with and convicted of commission of the crime.

A person is a party to a crime only if that person:

a. Directly commits the crime;

b. Intentionally helps in the commission of the crime;

c. Intentionally advises, encourages, hires, counsels, or procures another to commit the crime; or

d. Intentionally causes some other person to commit the crime under such circumstances that the other person is not guilty of any crime either in fact or because of legal incapacity.

Principal; Failure to Prosecute; Other Involved Persons

Any party to a crime who did not directly commit the crime may be indicted, tried, convicted, and punished for commission of the crime, on proof that the crime was committed and that the person was a party to it, even if the person accused of directly committing the crime has not been prosecuted or convicted, or has been convicted of a different crime or degree of crime, or is not amenable to justice, or has been acquitted.

Good Character of Defendant

When evidence of the good character of the defendant is offered, the jury has the duty to take that testimony, with all other evidence in the case, in determining the guilt or innocence of the defendant.

Good character is a positive, substantive fact and may be sufficient to produce in the minds of a jury a reasonable doubt about the guilt of the defendant. You have the duty to take any evidence of general good character with all the other evidence in the case, and if in doing so you should entertain a reasonable doubt about the guilt of the defendant, it would be your duty to acquit. However, if you should believe the defendant guilty beyond a reasonable doubt, you would be authorized to convict, in spite of the evidence about general good character.

Controlled Substances Act; Defined

A person commits the offense of possession or distribution of a controlled substance when they possess or transfer any quantity of a Schedule II drug as defined by Nita law anywhere in this state. I charge you that cocaine is a Schedule II drug under Nita law.

Verdict (Count 1)

If, after considering the testimony and evidence presented to you, together with the charge of the court, you should find and believe beyond a reasonable doubt that the defendant in Darrow County, Nita, did, on or about June 14, YR-2 commit the offense of Violation of the Controlled Substances Act as alleged in the indictment, you would be authorized to find the defendant guilty and, in that event, the form of your verdict would be: "We, the jury, find the defendant guilty."

Not Guilty Verdict Form

If you do not believe that the defendant is guilty or if you have any reasonable doubt as to the defendant's guilt, then it would be your duty to acquit the defendant, in which event the form of your verdict would be: "We, the jury, find the defendant not guilty."

Unanimous Verdict

Whatever your verdict is, it must be unanimous; that is, agreed on by all. The verdict must be signed by one of your members as foreperson, dated, and returned to be published in open court.

Responsibility for Sentencing

You are only concerned with the guilt or innocence of the defendant. You are not to concern yourselves with punishment.

Deliberations

One of your first duties in the jury room will be to select one of your number to act as foreperson, who will preside over your deliberations and who will sign the verdict to which all twelve of you freely and voluntarily agree.

You should start your deliberations with an open mind. Consult with one another and consider each other's views. Each of you must decide this case for yourself, but you should do so only after a discussion and consideration of the case with your fellow jurors. Do not hesitate to change an opinion if convinced that it is wrong. However, you should never surrender an honest opinion to be congenial or to reach a verdict solely because of the opinions of the other jurors.

Court Has No Interest in Case

By no ruling or comment that the court has made during the progress of the trial has the court intended to express any opinion on the facts of this case, the credibility of the witnesses, the evidence, or the guilt or innocence of the defendant.

IN THE SUPERIOR COURT OF DARROW COUNTY
STATE OF NITA

STATE OF NITA	)	
	)	
	)	
	)	INDICTMENT NUMBER: CR0287
v.	)	
	)	
	)	YR-0-CR0285
	)	
RICHARD CUNNINGHAM	)	
DEFENDANT	)	

VERDICT

COUNT 1

AS TO COUNT 1, WE THE JURY FIND THE DEFENDANT: ____________________

THIS _____ DAY OF _____, YR-_____.

____

FOREPERSON

Made in the USA
Coppell, TX
10 January 2024

27535741R00109